For Bob and Marilyn Bookchin

THE
MODERN CRISIS

Murray Bookchin

Published
in cooperation with
the Institute for Social Ecology
Rochester, Vermont

new society publishers
philadelphia, pa

304.2

Inquiries regarding requests to republish all or part of **The Modern Crisis** should be addressed to:

New Society Publishers
4722 Baltimore Avenue
Philadelphia, PA 19143

ISBN: 0-86571-084-8 Paperback
ISBN: 0-86571-083-X Hardcover

Printed in the United States

Cover Design by Brian Prendergast
Published in cooperation with the Institute for Social Ecology

New Society Publishers is a project of the New Society
Educational Foundation and a collective of the Movement for a
New Society. New Society Educational Foundation is a
nonprofit, tax-exempt, public foundation. Movement for a New
Society is a network of small groups and individuals working
for fundamental social change through nonviolent action. To
learn more about MNS, write: Movement for a New Society, 4722
Baltimore Avenue, Philadelphia, PA 19143. Opinions expressed
in this book do not necessarily represent positions of either the
New Society Educational Foundation or Movement for a New
Society.

Acknowledgements

I would like to express my appreciation to my closest colleagues at the Institute for Social Ecology, notably Daniel Chodorkoff, William Maclay, and Paul McIsaac. My dear friend John Clark has been a source of invaluable support and insights. I owe much to Howard Hawkins and John Ely for data, research materials, and many personal kindnesses in preparing this book.

Finally, I wish to thank Matt Becker of New Society Publishers for his many perceptive editorial suggestions and Jeanie Levitan for copyediting the entire manuscript.

Contents

Publisher's Note

The Chinese character for "crisis" is made up of two elements: "danger" and "opportunity." For those who want to change the world, *The Modern Crisis* is a challenging assessment of both.

But Murray Bookchin does not stop there. He spends little time cataloging the reasons for despair; nor does he present political solutions in terms of the hoped-for final results. I don't think Murray even believes in "final" results. The focus of *The Modern Crisis* is what questions we must ask to get from here to there, from a society which is destroying itself and its planet to a society which values its members and its environment enough to be sustainable.

This focus is anything but narrow. In this very short book, Murray considers social ecology, ethics, moral economics, municipally based democracy, and much more. Every page is food for thought for anyone interested in fundamental social change.

The Modern Crisis is not an easy read, but it rewards careful study. New Society Publishers is proud to publish it.

Matt Becker

About This Book

The essays in this book consist of lectures and articles that I prepared over the past three years. "Rethinking Ethics, Nature, and Society" was written specifically for *The Modern Crisis*. "What Is Social Ecology?" was presented as a lecture-seminar at the University of Frankfurt in November, 1984, and printed in the German radical monthly *Kommune*. "Market Economy or Moral Economy?" is based on a keynote address I gave at the annual convocation of the New England Organic Farmers' Association in June, 1983. "An Appeal for Social and Ecological Sanity" was written as a pamphlet for the Institute for Social Ecology in May, 1983.

> Murray Bookchin
> Director Emeritus
> Institute for Social Ecology
> Burlington, Vermont

Rethinking Ethics, Nature, and Society

The four articles that make up *The Modern Crisis* are guided by the view that our ideas and our practice must be imbued with a deep sense of ethical commitment. We must recover an image of the public good in a world that increasingly makes its choices between one "lesser evil" and another. Such an endeavor, which I plan to elaborate in a forthcoming book, *The Ethics of Evil*, can easily slip into self-righteous sermonizing if we do not examine certain basic assumptions that so distinctly mark the present era.

Most of the "isms" we have inherited from the past—liberalism, socialism, syndicalism, communism, capitalism—are rooted in the crude notion that human beings act almost exclusively from self-interest. This notion unites such widely disparate and immensely influential thinkers as Adam Smith, Karl Marx, and Sigmund Freud, not to speak of a huge bouquet of liberals, socialists, and self-styled "libertarians" (more properly proprietarians, the acolytes of Ayn Rand) in a common vision of human motivation and social behavior. Somewhere in the bowels of the Enlightenment and the Victorian era that followed it, ethical approaches to freedom, self-consciousness, and harmony began to give way to appeals for a "scientific," presumably "materialist," approach to a social reality grounded in egotism and the picture of a self-serving, indeed, avaricious human nature. Even so libertarian a visionary as Mikhail Bakunin, the fiery voice of nineteenth-century anarchism, echoes Marx and many radicals of his day when he militantly declares that "Wealth has always been and still is the indispensable condition for the realization of everything human...."[1] Let there be no mistake that these words are directed simply against any particular body of ideology or dogma. They reflect a widely accepted tendency in ideas that steadily reduced earlier pleas for freedom to "ideological" expressions of (read: apologias for) free trade; pleas for consciousness to "mystified" expressions of class interest; and ideals that called for a harmonious world to attempts to conceal a "historical" need for social discord—whether in the form of swashbuckling competition in the economic sphere or armed conflict in the social sphere.

What deeply disturbs me is the extent to which this image is so integrally part of our prevailing market economy—the profit-oriented capitalistic world men like Bakunin and Marx so earnestly opposed. The "embourgeoisment" of the working class, which troubled Bakunin in the 1870s, has expanded to embrace virtually all the radical "isms" we have inherited from the last century. Our bourgeois society has carried its own ideological baggage, filled with notions of self-interest, into the mental world of its opponents.

As a result, traditional radicalism in nearly all its

forms has become the alter ego of traditional capitalism. In a social universe where rival ideologies—be they conservative, liberal, or radical—root seemingly conflicting interpretations of social development in egotism, we are faced by a good deal more than the problem of ideological and psychological cooptation. The power of self-interest, whether we choose to call it "class interest" or private interest, becomes so much a part of the received wisdom of our period that it unconsciously shapes all our ideological premises. Causes like "socialism," "liberalism," or even "anarchism" become wedded to a distinctly bourgeois outlook in its crudest and most elemental sense even as they try to advance ideals that serve the public welfare.

The practical results of these assumptions are insidiously corrosive. Not only is every moral challenge to self-interest indulgently dismissed as "naive," "idealistic," and "utopian," but many people who are principled opponents of the prevailing order easily slip into "strategies" that appeal to specific interests in their crassest forms. "Bread-and-butter" issues, important as they surely are, are given almost embarrassing priority over moral and even long-range material ones. Thus the runaway growth that threatens to undermine the environment, the centralization of power that inches society toward an authoritarian State, and increases in armaments production that create jobs at the expense of the community's autonomy from the Pentagon are sanctified by the immediate needs of workers for employment.

A cozy adaptiveness to the seeming imperatives of "realism" is widely prevalent among people who avow a moral adherence to freedom. Radicalism becomes radically schizophrenic: a fragile, unworldly life of ideals coexists with a stolid, very worldly practice spawned by opportunism. The hidden agenda, with its visible "superstructure" composed of pitches to self-interest and concealed "base" of lofty principles reserved for private discussion—a "just-between-us" kind of socialism and liberalism that presumably balances out a public life of manipulative calculation—becomes the rule of our time. Given this chasm between principle and practice, we can justly ask what has happened to the "self" that structures its ideology and activities around self-interest on the one hand and an emancipatory self-consciousness on the other. The modern crisis, in effect, includes a serious crisis in radicalism itself and in many ideological movements that try to resolve the dislocations of our time.

Any project that seeks to deal with this crisis must also be a project that rehabilitates the prevailing image of human motivation. Indeed, it is an endeavor that must go still further: it must try to separate radicalism (or, if you choose, the liberatory movement in all its forms) from its deep roots in our market society and the vicious mentality it breeds. Whether in socialism, anarchism, or liberalism, moral issues must be raised again to remove a toxic legacy of realpolitik that has shunted them aside from their centrality in struggles for human emancipation. I know of nothing more warped than attempts to come to terms with a thoroughly irrational "reality" and a "realism" that increasingly asks us to choose between the alternatives of nuclear immolation and ecological disaster. This dilemma, which is the height of *unreality* in Hegel's famous equation of the "real" with the "rational," forms the "big picture" of our time, or what sociologists pompously call its "macro-problems." Entering deeply into the factors that have produced the dilemma is a moral issue: the conviction that every benefit must be "purchased" by a risk—in short, that for every "advance" humanity must pay a penalty. Why this should be so remains inexplicable unless good is indissolubly wedded to evil, in which case ethics conceived as a pursuit of virtue becomes a contradiction in terms.

What this "benefit-versus-risk" formula has produced, however, is a monumental apologia for all the ills of our time, a justification for the existence of evil as such and its entry into the core of life in the modern world. When good and bad are no longer placed in opposition to each other but rather adjusted to *coexist* with each other as though they were integrally part of the same phenomenon, ethical standards dissolve into techniques for accommodation to things as they are.

Even a moral movement to redeem movements for social change becomes a mere problem of calculation—specifically, of the risks we must incur in matters of principle in exchange for the benefits we wish to gain in matters of practice. This is a typical bourgeois calculation which every entrepreneur faces when he or she enters the marketplace jungle, a calculation that has become an issue in ethics precisely because moral behavior in the marketplace is all but impossible. That a "benefit-versus-risk" mentality has become the common coin of everyday discourse attests to the all-pervasiveness of a market economy. It exists no less in modern radicalism than in modern commerce. In both cases, the sweet smell of success, however opportunistically achieved, tends to win over the odium of possible failure in matters of principle.

There is a cruel, indeed, ironic justice to this calculation. Each risk that a benefit incurs, each "lesser evil" bought at the expense of principle, ultimately yields a universe of risks and evils that by far surpasses the original pair of choices that lead us to this ill-conceived strategy. In politics, Weimar Germany between World War I and II provides us with the classic example of this ethical devolution. Faced with paired choices of "lesser evils" or "benefits-versus-risks" from one election to another, German Social Democracy played a gamble with destiny that led it from the prospect of revolution, which it unscrupulously aborted, to choices between a moderate Left and a tolerant Center, a tolerant Center and an authoritarian Right, and finally an authoritarian Right and totalitarian Fascism. The results, of course, are history, a history presumably tucked away in the past. But the strategy is painfully contemporary. In daily life, this devolution is an ongoing process that has become so automatic that it no longer appears to be a matter of choice. So complete is the surrender of ethics to the mere process of functioning, of principle to the mere routine of survival, that it has become an unthinking series of operations at the most molecular level of life.

One can easily blame people for becoming caricatures of their lost humanity. Everyday life has steadily acquired almost bovine characteristics. Society is little more than a pasture and people a herd grazing on a diet of trivialities and petty pursuits. The price we pay for this repellent reduction of humans to domesticated, shepherded, and unthinking beings is costly beyond imagination. The insults our elites inflict on their subordinates by cajoling them do not solve the problems of our times, but simply remove them from public purview.

Hence, the reinstatement of an ethical stance becomes central to the recovery of a meaningful society and a sense of selfhood, a realism that is in closer touch with reality than the opportunism, lesser-evil strategies, and benefit-versus-risk calculations claimed by the practical wisdom of our time. Action from principle can no longer be separated from a mature, serious, and concerted attempt to resolve our social and private problems. The highest realism can be attained only by looking beyond the given state of affairs to a vision of what *should* be, not only what *is*. The crisis we face in human subjectivity as well as human affairs is so great, and its received wisdom is so anemic, that we literally will not *be* if we do not realize our potentialities to be more than we are.

The scope of the modern crisis is reconnoitered in the pieces that make up this book. My intention here is not to review the problems that have formed it. That would be redundant. I would like now, however, to examine their depths and their connections to each other, to go beneath the surface of the book and explore certain cohering thoughts from which we can develop a meaningful whole.

If we desperately need an ethics that will join the ideal with the real and give words like "realism" a richer, more rational meaning than they have, then we are faced with a traditional dilemma. How can we objectively validate ethical claims in an era of moral relativism when good and bad, right and wrong, virtue and evil, even the selection of strategies for social change are completely subjectivized into matters of taste or opinion? The overstated claim that what is good for a highly personalized "me" may not be good for an equally personalized "you" speaks to the growing amorality of our time. Accordingly, such a moral relativism (I can hardly call it a relativistic "ethics" without debasing the very meaning of the word ethics) has acquired the sanctity of a constitutional precept in our system of government. It has become the standard by which to determine the criminality of behavior and the guiding principles of diplomacy, religion, politics, and education, not to mention business and personal affairs. The subjectivization of behavioral precepts reflects the universal opportunism of the time; its emphasis is on operational ways of life as distinguished from philosophical ones, especially on ways to survive and function, rather than on ideals imbued with meaning.

That moral relativism can deliver us to a totally noncritical view of a world in which mere taste and fleeting opinion justify anything, including nuclear immolation, has been stressed enough not to require further elucidation. If mere opinion suffices to validate social behavior, then the social order itself can be validated simply by public opinion polls. Hence, whether capital punishment is "right" or "wrong" ceases to be an ethical question about the sanctity of life. The issue becomes a problem of juggling percentages, which may justify the slaughter of homicidal felons during one year and their right to live during another. Whether the figures of our polls go up or down can decide whether a given number of people will be put to death or not. Carried to its logical conclusion, this personalistic, operational view of morality can justify a totalitarian society, which abolishes the very claims of the individual. It was not from a sense of irony or perversity that visitors to Mussolini's Italy in the twenties applauded a fascist regime because Italian trains operated on time. The efficiency of a social system and mere matters of personal convenience were identified with its claims to be the embodiment of the public welfare.

To exorcise moral relativism, with its distasteful extensions into a politics of lesser-evils and a practice structured around risk-versus-benefit calculations, is a vexing problem indeed. The converse of a radical moral relativism is a radical moral absolutism which can be as totalitarian in its power to control as its relativistic opposite is democratic in its power to relax. Both live in a curious intellectual symbiosis: the seeming pluralism of a moral democracy has been known to encompass a fascistic ethics as easily as an anarchic one—which raises the question of how to keep a democracy from voting itself out of existence.

Suffice it to say that moral absolutism is neither better nor worse than the *concrete* message it has to offer. An ethics grounded in ecology can yield a salad of "natural laws" that are as tyrannical in their conclusions as the chaos of a moral relativism is precariously wayward. To appeal from ecology to God is to leap from nature to supernature, that is, ironically, from the human subject as it exists in the real world to the way it exists in the imagination. Religious precepts are the products of priests and visionaries, not of an objective world from which we can gain a sense of ethical direction that is neither the commanding dicta of "natural law" on the one hand nor supernatural "law" on the other. We have learned only too well that Hitler's "blood and soil" naturism, like Stalin's cosmological "dialectics," can be used as viciously as notions of "natural law" (with all their Darwinian connotations of "fitness to survive" and "natural selection") to collect millions of people in concentration camps, where they are worked to death, incinerated, or both.

Indeed, the suspicion surrounding the choice of nature as a *ground* for ethics is justified by a history of nature philosophies which gave validity to oligarchy (Plato), slavery (Aristotle), hierarchy (Aquinas), necessity (Spinoza), and domination (Marx), to single out the better-known thinkers of western philosophy.* Rarely indeed has nature itself been seen as a nascent domain of freedom, selfhood, and consciousness. Almost invariably, western thinkers have dealt with the natural world as a

---

*Let me emphasize the word "ground" and point out that I do not use the word "source," which has been carelessly tagged onto my views. Ethics presupposes the presence of volition, the intellectual ability to conceptualize and the social ability to *institutionalize* communities, not merely to *collect* into a community. These capacities are uniquely human and deserve emphasis as such, all the more because certain environmentalists tend to ignore humanity's uniqueness as a potentially rational and social animal in the sense that I use the word "social." Nature does not have will in the human sense of the term, nor does it possess the power of conceptualization. The sense in which nature is a ground for ethics, not ethical *as such*, will be explored shortly.

wilderness that has always been hostile to humanity or controlled by "natural law," a lawfulness unerring in its necessitarian relationships.

It is here that social ecology fills a void in an objective ethics that is neither absolutist nor relativist, authoritarian nor chaotic, necessitarian nor arbitrary—with all the pitfalls for humanity that these paired notions have yielded. Given social ecology's emphasis on nature's fecundity, on its thrust toward increasing variety, on its limitless capacity to differentiate life-forms and its development of richer, more varied evolutionary pathways that steadily involve ever more complex species, our vision of the natural world begins to change. We no longer need look upon it as a necessitarian, withholding, or "stingy" redoubt of blind "cruelty" and harsh determinism. Although never a "realm of freedom," nature is not reducible to an equally fictitious "realm of necessity," as earlier philosophers, social thinkers, and scientists claimed. The possibility of freedom and individuation is opened up by the rudimentary forms of self-selection, perhaps even "choice," if you will, of the most nascent and barely formed kind that emerges from the increasing complexity of species and their alternate pathways of evolution. Here, without doing violence to the facts, we can begin to point to a thrust in evolution that contains the potentialities of freedom and individuation. Here, too, we can see certain premises for social life—conceived, to be sure, as the institutionalization of the animal community into a potentially rational, self-governing form of association—and, owing to the ever-greater complexity of the nervous system and brain, for the emergence of reason itself.

This ensemble of ideas, I submit, provides us with the basis for an ecological ethics which sees the emergence of selfhood, reason, and freedom *from* nature—not in sharp opposition *to* nature. Natural evolution over time gives rise from within itself to a rich wealth of gradations that open the way to social evolution—in short, two evolutionary pathways in which one is parent to the other. The traditional dualism in human thought that pitted humanity against animality, society against nature, freedom against necessity, mind against body, and, in its most insidious hierarchical form, man against woman is transcended by due recognition of the continuity between the two, but without a reductionism or "oneness" that yields, in Hegel's words, "a night in which all cows are black."[2] This transcendence is achieved *historically*, not by arguing out the problem from within the trenches of biology and society—as though each can be discussed and explored separately from the other—and then constructing some kind of mechanical apparatus to "bridge" the gap between these dualities. With the use of an evolutionary approach to explain the evolution of humanity out of animality, society out of nature, and mind out of body, we shed sociobiology's tyrannical "morality of the gene." We also free ourselves from antihumanism's reductionist dissolution of human uniqueness into a cosmic "community" in which ants are equatable to people, from the infamous "lifeboat ethic" that denies the need to share the means of life with others who are less privileged, from an overtly National Socialist outlook that validates the authority of self-appointed "supermen" to dominate "subhumans," and from a Stalinist reduction of human beings to the raw material of a "History" governed by the inexorable "laws" of dialectical materialism.

Let me emphasize that social ecology, while viewing nature as a ground for an ethics of freedom and individuation, does not see an inexorable "lawfulness" at work that derives the human from the nonhuman or society from nature. Social ecology is not only a philosophy of process, it is also a philosophy of potentiality. Potentiality involves a sensitivity to the latent possibilities that inhere in a given constellation of phenomena, not a surrender to predetermined inevitability. It is the capability "to be" that is not as yet in being, a process in which the conditions for a specific line of development exist but have yet to achieve fruition as a "whole" with all its wealth of fullness, self-development, and uniqueness. Analogies more often tell us what this approach to reality is than propositional elucidations: the acorn, for example, which has the potentiality to become an oak tree or the human embryo which has the potentiality to become a fully mature and creative adult. This notion, in any case, is a message of freedom, not of necessity; it speaks to an immanent striving for realization, not to a predetermined certainty of completion. What is potential in an acorn that yields an oak tree or in a human embryo that yields a mature, creative adult is equivalent to what is potential in nature that yields society and what is potential in society that yields freedom, selfhood, and consciousness.

I find it odd that social ecology—the most organic

of our social disciplines—is often discussed in strictly reductionist and analytical terms. Indeed, there is a strong tendency to *collect* ideas rather than *derive* them, to disassemble or reassemble them as though we were dealing with an automobile engine, rather than explore them as aspects of a process. If recent cosmological theories about the universe are sound, the notion that it originated from a pulse of energy does not mean that all "matter" can henceforth be reduced to energy. Rather, the ecological thrust of that originating pulse has been to elaborate and differentiate itself, forming subatomic, atomic, molecular, and finally, richly elaborated and ever more complex inorganic and organic forms. Moreover, without introducing any notion of predetermination and teleology into our ways of thinking, each form can best be understood as emerging out of its predecessor—the later and more complex generally incorporating the earlier and simpler ones, whether internally or as part of a community.

This biological or organic way of thinking—which in no way conflicts with the proper use of mechanical or analytical forms of thought but rather *encompasses* them—is strangely lacking in many socially oriented schools of ecology. I still encounter schools which tend simply to inventory energy on one side and "matter" on an opposing side instead of deriving the latter from the former. Similarly, biocentric values are opposed to anthropocentric, the objective world of things is opposed to the subjective world of ideas, the strictly natural is opposed to the strictly social. We would do well to ask if they are in conflict with, or reducible to, each other—indeed, if we are thinking about them in a thoroughly rounded manner when we render them so one-sidedly and simplistically. Even the "horrid" words "anthropocentricity" and "humanism," so disdained these days by many socially oriented ecologists, raise the question of whether human beings have their own special place in nature with all their uniqueness and their own distinctive contribution to the whole.

We are very much in need of organic, more precisely, really dialectical ways of process-thinking that seek out the potentiality of a later form in an earlier one, that seek out the "forces" that impel the latter to give rise to the former, and that absorb the notion of process into truly evolutionary ways of thought about the world. Until this organic mode of thought is brought to ecophilosophy and applied in a sensitive, richly nuanced, and rounded manner, our attempts to reflect deeply on ecological problems will tend to be painfully superficial and incomplete.*

I can give no "definition" of social ecology that excludes the totality of these concepts, unified by the process that produces them. Just as Herbert Marcuse "defined" capitalism as all that appears and

---

*This is as good a place as any to point out that process-thinking of this kind is meaningless without empirical verification of our conclusions in the real world. But an empirical test of our ideas cannot be an attempt to test a fixed set of ideas with a fixed set of facts, as the acolytes of common sense and a crude pragmatism would have us believe. In truly dialectic thinking, an empirical test must explore whether a given *process* in its theoretical form explains a given *process* in real life. That processes in thought must try to explain processes in reality is a basic notion of empirical verification that has eluded even many self-professed "dialecticians" and left them open to compelling criticisms by pragmatists and positivists.

is worked out in the three volumes of Marx's *Capital* (and, I would be inclined to say, a good deal more), so social ecology is what I have tried to detail in the passages above and a good deal more. At a time when social ecology, once a rarely used term which I chose to express the ideas contained in this book, is being bounced around in an increasing number of publications, it would be well to bear its specific meaning in mind. To divest this term of its liberatory, processual, and ethical content is to completely hybridize utterly antithetical concepts. Our age, which faces intellectual suffocation because of a massive denaturing of language into "buzz words" and a degradation of concepts into simplistic "definitions," is guided by cheap academic fashions as well as by media-created fads. To resist this melding of words and concepts into a goulash of ideas is to resist the degradation of mind itself. Given the unabated production of fashions, fads, "buzz words," and superficial ideas, we have compelling reasons to fear for our spiritual degradation as well as our ecological degradation.

The very word *social* that is added to the word ecology—in contrast to the more commonly used term, "human ecology"—is meant to emphasize that we can no more separate society from nature than we can separate mind from body. If nature provides the ground for an ethics that has an objective ancestry in evolution's thrust toward freedom, selfhood, and reason, so too nature provides the ground for the emergence of society. Here again we must exhibit the utmost delicacy in the treatment of ideas. Animal communities are not societies. Whatever else they have, they do not form those uniquely human contrivances we call institutions, which systematically and often purposively organize relationships among people along kinship lines in tribal societies, political ones in cities, and statist ones in nations and empires. Just as we must presuppose the emergence of municipal institutions that in classical Athens produced the *polis* or so-called city-state, a community that gave due recognition to an extraordinarily intelligent figure like Pericles, so we must presuppose the emergence of national institutions that gave virtually absolute power to idiots like Louis XVI of France and Nicholas II of Russia. In either case, the leadership and power conferred on these individuals had little to do with their physical strength (the usual source of so-called dominance in animal groups) and, with the exception of Pericles, their mental capacities. Rather, their authority came from well-organized, carefully structured, and historically developed agencies: armies, bureaucracies, police, or, in Athens' case, a large "town meeting" called the *ecclesia*.

We encounter nothing like these agencies in the animal world. The so-called castes we find among "social" insects like bees and termites are genetic in origin, not contrived. By their rigidity they are fixed in ways that stand sharply at odds with human forms of organization, which are repeatedly altered by reforms or simply overthrown by revolutions.

The ways in which human societies have an ancestry in animal communities are too complex to examine here. One thing should be clarified, however: the two are not the same. Indeed, with the elaboration of human societies beyond the most elementary forms of scavenging and food gathering, we can see the emergence in humanity of two societies: the sororal society of women and the fraternal society of men. Perhaps the most underlying factor that makes for this duality in tribal communities is a division of *functions*—not simply a division of "labor." For it is more than work that separates the sexes into two fairly delineable social groups: it is culture itself. Women and men develop their own distinctive lifeways, modes of expression, behavioral traits, values, rituals, sensibilities, even deities, myths, and traditions, as well as styles of work, not only forms of work. Home, garden, cleaning, food preparation, parenting, and many other functions constitute a complete domain that is distinctively a woman's realm. Man's domain consists of hunting, "politics" (to misuse a word that requires explanation), and, where it exists, the men's house, into which all the males withdraw after puberty to form a separate community of their own.

The two societies have existed, whether in well-developed or virtually vestigial form, from time immemorial. Initially, they were in a reasonable balance with each other, a balance that was notable for the absence of domination by either sex. Only later do we begin to encounter a relationship marked by male dominance. Hence hierarchy, where it existed at an early point in social development, was the exception rather than the rule. Difference, I must emphasize, must not be mistaken for dominance or submission, a problem that continually recurs in a world that organizes all differentia into an order of "one-to-ten" in everyday life and institutionalizes them into a "chain of command" in social and economic areas of life.

We also have a difficult time recognizing the very existence of these two societies and are even more troubled in our search for the precise reason "why" men came to dominate women. Accordingly, we look for gimmicks that explain this shift from equality between the sexes—an equality whose existence is often denied—to a condition clearly marked by male domination or the prevalence of a "man's world." The mechanical, often reductionist, nature of these explanations is found most clearly in the view advanced by Dorothy Dinnerstein, notably, that women who provide succor for children are also the earliest source of denial to them. Some of Dinnerstein's admirers, carrying this view to its extremes, argue that the feelings of denial that stem from woman's "monopoly of parenting" turn her into an object of hatred as well as love, and that this can be relieved by shared parenting by men and women. I find this explanation of misogyny, patriarchy, and even hierarchy highly questionable. It is not only too simplistic and reductionist, but also fails to account for the many variations in women's status that appear in societies where women continue to exercise a "monopoly of parenting" and, by any standards, are often far more loved by the young than are their fathers.

We come, here, to a highly revealing prejudice in the way our society today looks at the past, a difference that highlights the distinction between ecological and conventional ways of assessing human development. Underlying the widespread notion that woman has always lived in a "man's world" is a distinct bias that raises the male realm of civil society over woman's domestic world. Nourished by the enormous influence politics and statecraft have had on modern thinking, we tend to assume that civil society is always more important than domestic society, that "affairs of state" have primacy over the affairs of the household.

In tribal societies, this prejudgement of what is important and what is not is often pure fiction. Woman, whose food gathering and gardening activities often provide as much as eighty percent of the biomass consumed by hunter-gatherer societies, enjoys an economic eminence that certainly equals or even exceeds that of men. If we bear in mind that band and tribal communities are mainly domestic societies, the enormous importance we assign to civil society is largely a modern prejudice. Indeed, one could advance very persuasive arguments to support the claim that these societies were originally a "woman's world" and that women enjoyed a status that was "superior" to that of men.

Actually, we have no reason to suppose that the preeminence of a "woman's world" over a man's was marked by the dominance of females over males. Notions of dominance and submission have a very checkered history, even when applied to animals, that cannot be unravelled here. It is my own conviction that the *expansion* of the male's civil sphere, not its *a priori* supremacy at the very beginnings of the development of human social forms, explains the increasing supremacy of men over women—a view, I may add, that does not exclude the operation of many complex psychological, possibly even biological, factors. These may have reinforced patriarchy, but they do not in themselves explain "why" it emerged. It seems more likely, in my view, that civil society began to encroach upon domestic society and increasingly produce a "man's world" because of population pressure, the evolution of warfare (itself a very complex process), technological changes, and the slow reworking of early egalitarian societies by the elders of the community, its shamans, and, perhaps most decisively, its warriors. History itself, and the narrative it unfolds for us, are no less causal explanations than psychological gimmicks like a "monopoly of parenting" or hormonal drives.

The fallacies that the problem of male domination has generated, however, are significant indicators of the biases that interfere with an open study of social development. Difference, it cannot be emphasized often enough, *does not by itself yield hierarchy* or even a certain measure of dominance. The existence of two societies—male and female—does not justify a conclusion that one exercised supremacy over another. Finally, the fact that the male's civil society did achieve supremacy over the female's does not mean that it had to do so. The ability of social ecology to distinguish differentiation from domination, indeed, to visualize variation as part of wholeness rather than pyramidally, raises an important alternative. It opens the way to a sensibility that emphasizes harmony over antagonism and fosters a life-affirming ethics, objectively grounded in a fecund nature, that places a premium on variety, uniqueness and the ability of life forms to complement each other in forming richer and ever-creative wholes.

That hierarchy and domination did develop is another thesis, largely implied, that runs through the articles in this book. But here, too, we encounter problems that reveal an appalling wrongheadedness: the tendency, generated by so many liberals and Marxists, to anchor all relations in self-interest and economic motivation. I refer to the reduction of hierarchy to classes and of domination to exploitation. Hierarchy has a much broader meaning than class, a strictly economic relationship that Marx, quite properly, rooted in the ownership of property, the control of technology, and the various ways of operating the means of production. What is important, indeed crucial, about this distinction is that hierarchy preceded the emergence of classes and may long survive them if we are not mindful of its far-reaching implications. Hierarchy goes beyond the workplace into the very cradle, so to speak, indeed, into the socializing process, where infants are taught to deal with "otherness" as potentially hostile, as "objects" to be controlled. It is the breeding ground of those primary distinctions based on gender that are inculcated in the young. Finally, it teaches the young to accept their place in a social pyramid that reaches from the family to the summits of their adult lives. Not only are families, peer groups, educational institutions, religious centers, and the community at large schools for hierarchy as they are now constituted, so, too, are the workplace and, in no small part, the technologies that place people in their service. A classless society may emerge that poses no challenge to any of these social forms; a nonhierarchical society, challenging the most archetypal components of social life, indeed, the socializing process itself, goes much further. It poses the need to alter every thread of the social fabric, including the way we experience reality, before we can truly live in harmony with each other and with the natural world.

By the same token, domination preceded exploitation and may long survive an exploitative society if we are not mindful of its scope. Here, too, we must go far beyond the economic areas and economic relationships to search out sensibilities that seek to control all aspects of the world. The complexity of domination is such that even love, when used to manipulate and control, can produce submission as effectively as outright physical coercion. Indeed, self-domination, working through mechanisms like guilt and a variety of socialization techniques, has brought women, the young, and ethnic groups into complicity with their rulers more effectively than explicit methods of control. This again raises the need to go beyond the traditional "isms" structured around self-interest and economic motivations into the deepest recesses of the self: its formation in a cauldron of competition and conflicting interests whereby individuality is identified with domination, self-development with a mentality formed by rivalry, maturity with adaptation to things as they exist, success with acquisition and the sanctity of the bargain.

Social ecology provides the patterning forms to compare and alter the ensembles of hierarchy and domination that afflict us. Its ecological image of animal-plant communities, or what I prefer to call ecocommunities rather than ecosystems (with its bias for systems theory), challenges the notion that hierarchy exists between species. To designate lions as "kings" and ants as "lowly" is meaningless from an ecological viewpoint: ants, in fact, are far less dispensable in recycling an ecocommunity than lions, and words like "kingly" or "lowly" are extrapolations of our own social relationships into the natural world. As to intraspecific "hierarchies," they are so different in kind, so patently unequal to each other, and so transitory where they seem to exist at all, that a sizable volume would be needed to critically examine them with reasonable thoroughness. Suffice it to say that an elephant cow or "matriarch" who seems to lead a herd stands very much at odds with a baboon "patriarch." And a "queen" bee is simply an essential part of a reproductive organ we call a beehive, not a link in an institutionalized dynasty.*

An ecological society is more than a society that tries to check the mounting disequilibrium that exists between humanity and the natural world. Reduced to simple technical or political issues, this anemic view of such a society's function degrades the issues raised by an ecological critique and leads to purely

---

*These analogies and the thoughts behind them have been so freely lifted from my writings, generally with minimal or no acknowledgement, that the reader should be mindful of where they initially originated and the contexts in which they originally appeared. My concern is not simply with the problem of plagiarism; rather, I am much more troubled by the way they are used to support ideologies with which I differ profoundly, such as notions of "natural law" that provide a warrant to use authoritarian methods for the correction of ecological dislocations. In view of the libertarian message of social ecology, I find this hybridization of ideas very disturbing. I feel that a cautionary note should be made in the interests of freedom and clarity of ideas.

technical and instrumental approaches to ecological problems. Social ecology is, first of all, a *sensibility* that includes not only a critique of hierarchy and domination but a reconstructive outlook that advances a participatory concept of "otherness" and a new appreciation of differentiation as a social and biological desideratum. Formalized into certain basic principles, it is also guided by an ethics that emphasizes variety without structuring differences into a hierarchical order. If I were to single out the precepts for such an ethics, I would be obliged to use two words that give it meaning: participation and differentiation.

Social ecology is largely a philosophy of participation in the broadest sense of the word. In its emphasis on symbiosis as the most important factor in natural evolution, this philosophy sees ecocommunities as participatory communities. The compensatory manner by which animals and plants foster each other's survival, fecundity, and well-being surpasses the emphasis conventional evolutionary theory places on their "competition" with each other—a word that, together with "fitness," is riddled with ambiguities. Competition may accurately describe the workings of our capitalist market, but it does not include the more meaningful principle of complementarity—which, alas, some "natural law" acolytes have decided to call a "law"—that describes the mutualistic interaction of animals and plants.

Similarly, differentiation not only emphasizes the importance of variety for ecological stability, but is also the all-important context for the eventual emergence of a nascent freedom in an ecocommunity. Complexity, a product of variety, is a crucial factor in opening alternative evolutionary pathways. The more differentiated the life-form and the environment in which it exists, the more acute is its overall sensorium, the greater its flexibility, and the more active its participation in its own evolution.

The two concepts cannot be raised without leading to interaction with each other. The greater the differentiation, the wider is the degree of participation in elaborating the world of life. An ecological ethics not only affirms life, it also focuses on the *creativity* of life.

These concepts extend from nature directly into society. They provide us with principles that overcome the dualism between nature and society—not only in theory but also in practice. Looking back in time, we find that the history of society deliciously grades out of the history of life without either being subsumed by the other. Our earliest institutions were based on blood ties, age groups, and gender functions—all biological facts, yet distinctively social in that natural affinities are given structure and stability, cohered by ideologies, and expanded to include seemingly "alien" groups through marital exogamy and the exchange of gifts. In time, the emergence of early cities expands the social bond to a point where people see themselves not only as kin, but also as a common species—a universal *humanitas*. The idea of citizenship, while never completely supplanting the family tie, opens a new community arena and a wide range of human intercourse. A continuum can be traced from the simplest kinds of biological association between human beings to an ever-expansive social arena that fosters participation and, with it, greater differentiation in functions, institutional forms, and individual personalities. Participation unites the biotic ecocommunity with the social ecocommunity by opening new evolutionary possibilities in nature and society. Differentiation yields richer possibilities for the elaboration of these ecocommunities and adds the dimension of freedom, however nascent in nature or explicit in society.

It is at this point that social ecology becomes overtly *political*. Communities normally exist within communities: individual families within tribes, tribes within tribal confederations, confederations that create cities, and cities that enter into confederal relationships with each other. The problem we face is: Where did we leap out of scale to produce state institutions that began to work against participation and also inhibit differentiation? To put this question in more general terms: Where did we go wrong in our history such that we face a crisis of monumental proportions in our relationships with each other and with the natural world?

We clearly leaped out of scale when we formed the nation-state. And it is not only the scale on which we function that has exploded beyond our comprehension and control, but also the deep wound we have inflicted on our own humanity. Ordinary people find it impossible to participate in a nation: they can belong to it but it never belongs to them. The size of the nation-state renders active citizenship impossible, at least on the national level, and it turns politics, conceived as something more than a media spectacle, into a form of statecraft in which the citizen is increasingly disempowered by authoritarian executive agencies, their legislative minions, and an all-encompassing bureaucracy.

That politics, a Hellenic term that once meant the management of the *polis*, or municipality, in face-to-face assemblies and publicly controlled councils, is so far removed from our present experience that the word has acquired a sneeringly pejorative meaning need hardly be emphasized. "Politicians" cut shabby figures today; they are the objects of public mistrust and forbearance. The fact that this word was once a *municipal* term, applicable only to the *polis*, has been all but forgotten. The disempowerment of the citizen and the attribution of political activity lead ultimately to the attrition of the self. The real victim of the depoliticization of the people is the ego and human personality, through the transformation of citizens from publicly active human beings into atomized, trivialized "constituencies" who are preoccupied with their individual survival in a world over which they exercise no control. This wound is still hemorrhaging in the "body politic" and threatens to bleed people of all their humanity.

Going back further in time, we can see that we went wrong when the market system broke through the confines which traditional society established to contain it. Traditional societies had a genuine fear of unbridled commerce and the accumulation of wealth. They saw it as anti-social and demonic, a corrosive effluvium of greed and self-aggrandizement that threatened to dissolve long-established ties based on mutual aid and community welfare. This archaic insight has been proven out with a vengeance. Capitalism is a "system" (if such it can be called) that gives rise to the universal reign of limitless buying and selling, indeed, of limitless growth and expansion. The reduction of the citizen to a buyer and seller in the economic realm, not only a "constituent" in the political, carries marketplace rivalry into the most intimate everyday aspects of life. We not only engage in a "struggle with nature," but we also engage in a struggle with each other. Indeed, our struggle with each other is the source of our "struggle with nature," a fact that was to entrap both Marx and one of traditional anarchism's revered "fathers." In Marx's case, this ensemble of "struggles" gave rise to radical theories in which the emergence of class societies was seen as a desideratum and the bourgeoisie was cast as a "permanently revolutionary" class in the historic drama of "man's" ascent from "animality."[3] Capitalist ideology goes even further: it not only claims that freedom presupposes the "domination of nature," but it sees the "domination of nature" as an ongoing "struggle," a process of *social* selection in which the "fit" survive, no less in society than in nature, while those who cannot "succeed" in both realms fall by the wayside.

For a generation that has experienced the horrors of Auschwitz, the viciousness of this view would hardly require emphasis if it were not incorporated by implication—at times, even explicitly—into "natural-law" theory. Historically, it not only stands at odds with the value systems of all precapitalist societies, which emphasized the virtues of cooperation and giving, but also provides a ghastly apologia for the wounds that have been inflicted on the natural world. That trade was potentially evil and profit-making outright sin was a theme that ran through the morality of all precapitalist societies and served in great measure to block the ascendancy of early capitalist relationships over society as a whole. The cultural barriers that precapitalist societies raised against incipient forms of capitalism impeded the latter's development for thousands of years. It was not until the eighteenth century and primarily in England that capitalist market relations finally broke through these barriers and proceeded to spread like an aggressive cancer throughout the world.

My use of the word "cancer" is deliberate and literal, not merely metaphorical. Capitalism, I would argue, is the cancer *of* society—not simply a *social* cancer, a concept that implies it is some form of human consociation. It is not a social phenomenon but rather an economic one; indeed, it is the substitution of economy for society, the ascendancy of the buyer-seller relationship, mediated by things called "commodities," over the richly articulated social ties that past civilizations at their best elaborated and developed for thousands of years in networks of mutual aid, reciprocity, complementarity, and other support systems which made social life meaningful and humanizing. Like all uncontrollable cancers, capitalism has shown that it can grow indefinitely and spread into every social domain that harbored ties of mutuality and collective concern.

If there are any "limits" to the growth of capitalism, they are to be found not in any of its so-called internal contradictions, such as economic breakdown or class wars between the workers and bourgeoisie as so many radical economists tell us, but in the destruction of that host we call "society," the host which this cancer parasitizes and threatens to annihilate. To respond properly to this kind of crisis, we must develop not only specific antibodies that will arrest the disease, and admittedly the valuable palliatives that will slow up its growth, but also a new immunological system that will make society completely resistant to its recurrence. And I speak, here, of a *system* rather than a contrivance or "technological fix," so strongly favored by the so-called realists in the environmental movement—an ensemble of new sensibilities, cultural forms, a moral economy in which the word "economy" implies a recovery of the original Greek origin of the term as the management of the *oikos*, or household, and a new politics, which recovers its Greek definition as the management of the local community.

The culture and sensibility I call "ecological" is not the primary concern of this book. I have dealt with it in great detail in other works.* In any case, they can be inferred quite easily from my remarks on the ethical importance of dealing with the "other" in a complementary manner and the emphasis I place on participation and differentiation as the great motifs in organic evolution. The essays "What Is Social Ecology?" and "Market Economy or Moral Economy?" in fact are permeated by an ethical message that raises cultural and attitudinal solutions to the problems we face. My main concern, however, is to examine the ethical bases, to the extent that these exist in nature and the economy, for an

---

*See particularly *Post-Scarcity Anarchism*, which has recently been reprinted by Black Rose Books in Montreal, and my latest work, *The Ecology of Freedom* (Palo Alto: Cheshire Books, 1983). Readers may also care to consult *Toward An Ecological Society*, also published by Black Rose Books.

ecological politics. I am deeply concerned with what constitutes the proper domain for that kind of politics and the reconstructive steps that can be taken to remove in a creative way the causes that are leading to either ecological breakdown or a nuclear holocaust.

If we rely on self-interest and economic motives to evoke the popular response that will deal with these overarching problems, we will be relying on the very constellation of psychological factors that have so decisively contributed to their emergence. Here we encounter the ironic perversity of a "pragmatism" that is no different, in principle, from the problems it hopes to resolve. Nor can we rely on a politics of media manipulation and party mobilization that really hitches the "masses" to statecraft. Statecraft is for statesmen and the "politics" it generates turns the most dedicated idealists into sleazy politicians. This is not, to be sure, because of bad intentions, but rather because of the exigencies of power-brokering, parliamentarianism, and the inevitable effect of a puffed up, larger-than-life public imagery on ordinary mortals.

Are we obliged, then, to fall back on the good that exists in human nature? It is fashionable, today, to deprecate this element in political life, certainly in a society that assumes that human nature is at best a blank page on which the environment can inscribe anything, or at worst a malignant evil that must be kept in tow by coercion and fear. Yet let us not sell this factor short. Human beings exhibit more care, dedication, and love than most students of their psyches are willing to acknowledge. There is a great

deal of truth to Jules Michelet's description of the
French people during the opening months of their
great revolution and the sentiment that filled them—
a description, in fact, that one often encounters in
most hard-nosed, skeptical, and amoral historians of
other revolutions as well. "To attain unity," declares
the old historian of his country's revolutionary
rebirth, "nothing was able to prove an impediment,
no surprise was considered too dear. All at once, and
without even perceiving it, the [French people] have
forgotten the things for which they would have
sacrificed their lives the day before, their provincial
sentiments, local traditions, and legends. Time and
space, those material conditions to which life is
subject, are no more. A strange *vita nuova*, one
eminently spiritual, and making her revolution a sort
of dream, at one time delightful, at another terrible,
is now beginning for France. It knew neither time
nor space."[4]

Perhaps this is overstated. But there is enough truth
in it to say that historical moments do arrive when
human beings, collectively as well as singly, exhibit
a sense of solidarity, care, and dedication that goes
beyond mere inspiration to become a devout passion.
We would be hard put to explain how many
movements for moral regeneration—for example,
Christianity, Islam, Buddhism, or even various forms
of socialism—could be reduced to "material
interest," a Bakunin or a Marx notwithstanding.* The

---

*And I would emphasize that more than ever, today, we need a
new movement for moral reawakening, not only for meeting
human material needs—important as these are at all times. The
great failing of contemporary "Leftist" movements, be they
socialist or anarchist, is that a new society is conceived primarily
as one that places "bread and beef" on the table, with the ironic

cries of "Life, liberty, and the pursuit of happiness" and "Liberty, Equality and Fraternity," hollow as they may seem today in the ears of many self-styled "radicals," have a magnificent utopian dimension to them, a universal appeal that transcends the various conflicting interests that tried to manipulate the American and French revolutions for their own benefit. Indeed, it is doubtful if millions of people could have been set in motion, often exhibiting a stronger spirit of self-sacrifice than self-interest, if these appeals had spoken only to the economic concerns of calculating merchants and competitive capitalists. Even if one allows for the worst intentions of the few who used the good intentions of the many for their own private ends, the reality of these appeals consists in the empirical fact that the many *did* form the great majority of the people and *their* intentions made social change possible and tangible, however much it was perverted later on.

If we are to explore human nature, we cannot ignore certain features about it that justify a belief in its cooperative and life-affirming tendencies. Human beings are more helpless and dependent at birth than most animals; their development to maturity requires more time than their nearest primate cousins. This protracted period of development which makes for the mental ability of humans to form a culture also fosters a deep sense of interdependence that promotes the formation and stability of community.

result that the "Right" has gained the support of millions through moral appeals that give a sense of meaning to life in an increasingly meaningless society. I am thoroughly convinced that no new social movement will capture the imagination of people today without providing a sense of moral well-being, not only material well-being—indeed, of moral purpose, not only material improvement.

We are eminently social animals not because of instinct but rather because we must cooperate with each other to mature in a healthy fashion, not only to survive. This kind of cooperation, which involves a long period of parenting, indeed of touching and caressing, makes for a strong need to associate with others of our own kind. The worst punishment that can be inflicted on any normal human being is isolation, and the most serious emotional trauma the individual seems to suffer is separation. The love, care, aid, and goodwill that a group can furnish to an individual are perhaps the most important contribution it can make to an individual's ego development. Denied these supportive attentions, ego-formation, personal development, and individuality become warped. Speaking in ecological terms, the making of that "whole" we call a rounded, creative, and richly variegated human being crucially depends upon community supports for which no amount of self-interest and egotism is a substitute. Indeed, without these supports, there would be no real self to distort—only a fragmented, wriggling, frail, and pathological thing that could only be called a self for want of another word to describe it.

The making of a human being, in short, is a collective process, a process in which both the community and the individual *participate*. It is also a process which, at its best, evokes by its own variety of stimuli the wealth of abilities and traits within the individual that achieve their full degree of *differentiation*. The extent to which these individual potentialities are realized, the unity of diversity they achieve, and the scope they acquire depend crucially upon the degree to which the community itself is participatory and richly differentiated in the stimuli, forms, and choices it creates that make for personal self-formation. Denied the opportunity to participate in a community, whether because it is incomprehensibly large or socially exclusive, the individual begins to feel disempowered and ineffectual, with the result that his or her ego begins to shrivel. Divested of differentiated stimuli, opportunities, choices, and variegated groups that speak to his or her proclivities, the individual becomes a homogenized thing, passive, obedient, and privatized, which makes for a submissive personality and a manipulable constituent.

The principles of social ecology, structured around participation and differentiation, thus reach beyond the biotic ecocommunity directly into the social one, indeed, into the nature of the ego itself and the image it forms of the other. An ecological ethics of freedom thus coheres nature, society, and the individual into a unified whole that leaves the integrity of each untouched and free of a reductionist biologism or an antagonistic dualism. The social derives from the natural and the individual from the social, each retaining its own integrity and specificity through a process of ecological derivation. The great splits between nature and society and between society and individuality are thus healed. They are healed not by any bridge, a term that implies the existence of chasms that are crossed by a structure, but by the very *process* of derivation—that is, by the fact that the individual *is* the history of individuality as it emerges from society and society *is* the history of society as it emerges from natural history itself. So, too, is mind in its relationship to body, thought in relationship to physicality, the "I" in relationship to the "other," a liberatory, objective ethics in relationship to the nascent freedom that emerges in the natural world, and humanity in relationship to nature.

The ecological and eminently ethical principles advanced here open distinctly reconstructive avenues in our efforts to resolve the crisis created by ecological breakdown and a world that lives under the shadow of thermonuclear extinction. These avenues are the overarching thoughts in the latter half of my "An Appeal for Social and Ecological Sanity," and they need not be examined in detail here. One focal issue, however, would benefit from some elucidation: the centrality I give to libertarian municipalism.

Town, city, and neighborhood are the most intimate environments that extend beyond the home and the place of work. For the young and many women, they are often the only ones that exist. There was a time when the workplace was part of the immediate community and life was lived, as it still is in many places outside megalopolitan areas, in the immediate proximity of a person's household. The medieval town, like so many ancient ones, was intensely peopled; it was the object of firm, personal loyalties, the public sphere in an emotional as well as a political sense, the most important terrain for self-formation beyond the immediate family. Most importantly, it was the arena in which people empowered themselves in assemblies, publicly controlled councils, and in plazas, squares, and other gathering places where they could discuss and resolve public problems.

To be a "citizen" was not a legal abstraction, a juridical void to be filled by rules and regulations delivered by godlike powers far removed from one's personal horizon of the world. Citizenship connoted a high degree of participation, be it in face-to-face decisionmaking or administrative involvement. Politics, in effect, was the notion of community seen as *communizing*, actively interrelating in formal assemblies and informal discussions. To be political meant to be communal, not to be a politician—a creature set aside from the community to be chosen or "elected" for the Elect, who alone could rule and command. These privileged attributes belong to the statesman who engages in the business of "*the State*"—a special apparatus set aside from the community solely to sit at its top with the full weight of authority and control of the means of violence.

By contrast, the municipality formed an arena in its own right. It emerged out of the *social* world in which people engage in their private affairs to develop into a *political* world in which they engage in their public affairs. Historically, it preceded the state with its apparatus of police, soldiers, courts, jails, bureaucracies, and the like. This kind of machinery appeared in cities as well, but usually when they entered into periods of decline and paved the way for the emergence of the state.

If, as I believe, the municipality is increasingly becoming a battleground on which civic politics belligerently confronts state manipulation, this is due in no small measure to the fact that the state, until comparatively recent times, has never been able to *fully* claim the municipality as its own. Like precapitalist societies which blocked the emergence of capitalism with their strong grassroots traditions and entrenched cultural forms, the municipality opposed outright state control with its guilds, neighborhood associations, local societies, and a vast variety of de facto self-governing institutions like the revolutionary sections of Paris in 1793–94 and a host of community organizations in later periods. Municipal life, richly textured by family networks and popular organizations—many of which cut across class lines—has always been a human refuge from the homogenizing and dehumanizing effects of state bureaucracies. This inner cultural strength has made it the bulwark *par excellence* against the encroachment of the state on public life, not only today but also historically.*

If the state today, owing in great part to the expansion of the market economy, threatens to destroy this refuge, this means that the municipality is not only faced with the loss of its traditional identity, but also is becoming, by the sheer pressure of events, the most significant terrain for the struggle

---

*The transclass nature of municipal movements is most clearly revealed in Manuel Castell's brief analysis of the occupational background of arrested or deported Communards after the Paris Commune of 1871. It may be well to note that the Commune was universally regarded as a "working class" insurrection and "model" for a Marxist "proletarian dictatorship." Historical material on the opposition which the nation-state encountered from cities will be found in Chapter Six of my book, *Urbanization Without Cities*, to be published in late 1986 by Sierra Club Books. See Manuel Castell: *The City and the Grassroots* (Berkeley: University of California Press; 1983), pp. 16–17.

against the state. Historically, there is nothing new about this confrontation. Almost every major revolution has involved—indeed has often been—a conflict between the local community and the centralized state. And just as the centralized state means the nation-state, so the local community means the municipality—be it the village, town, city, or neighborhood. From the peasant wars in Germany during the 1520s, through the English, American, and French revolutions, including Parisian uprisings from the 1790s to 1871, what we see are local communities pitted against centralized state institutions—a persistent conflict that has yet to receive the attention it deserves. The demand for "local control" does not necessarily mean the parochialism and insularity that evoked so much opposition in Marx's writings. In the force field generated by an increasingly centralized state and increasingly resistant communities, the cry for greater municipal autonomy echoes demands for a new political culture marked by autonomy, relative self-sufficiency, and more open democratic institutions.

To speak in a more constructive vein, the municipality may well be the one arena in which traditional institutional forms can be reworked to replace the nation-state itself. The potential for a truly liberatory radicalism has always been inherent in the municipality; it forms the bedrock for direct political relationships, face-to-face democracy, and new forms of self-governance by neighborhoods and towns. To be sure, the municipality's capacity to play a historic role in changing society today depends on the extent to which it can shake off the state institutions that have infiltrated it: its mayoralty structure, civic bureaucracy, and its own professionalized monopoly on violence. Rescued from these institutions, however, it retains the historic materials and political culture that can pit it against the nation-state and the cancerous corporate world that threatens to digest social life as such.

Let us not deceive ourselves, however, in thinking that a libertarian municipal alternative to the nation-state is meaningful in one or only a few communities. Freedom is not achievable in a lasting form on the margins or in the pockets of society. Left to themselves, state institutions are much too powerful to permit isolated towns and cities to regain their political autonomy. The creativity of municipal politics will ultimately be tested when villages, towns, and cities manage to confederate with each other and form radically new social networks, perhaps on a county level to begin with, later on a regional, and ultimately on a nationwide level.

The possibility that authoritarian forms of coordination will emerge from free municipalities cannot be discounted or legislated away by mere goodwill and idealistic rhetoric. Only insofar as the coordination of municipalities is strictly *administrative* and effectuated by recallable, rotatable, and clearly mandated *deputies* of the people—not their "representatives"—drawn from the citizens assemblies of their own munici-palities can we say that it is structured along libertarian lines. *Policy*, in turn, would have to be the exclusive province of the assemblies, not of elected "legislators." Here, Rousseau's famous remarks about "representation" are as valid today as they were two centuries ago:

> Sovereignty, for the same reason as it makes it inalienable, cannot be represented. It lies essentially in the general will, and will does not admit of representation: it is either the same, or other; there is no intermediate possibility. The deputies of the people, therefore, are not and cannot be its representatives: they are merely its stewards, and can carry through no definitive acts. Every law the people has not ratified in person is null and void—is, in fact, not a law. The people of England regards itself as free: but it is grossly mistaken: it is free only during the election of members of parliament. As soon as they are elected, slavery overtakes it, and it is nothing.[5]

Viewed philosophically, the free municipality transforms an ecological ethics from the realm of precept into the realm of politics. The Greeks tried to do this in real life when Athens was conceived as an ethical compact between its citizens, not merely as a dwelling place. Social ecology, which tries to plant its feet in nature, begins to raise its head in the municipality that is truly participatory and fosters differentiation—in short, that is truly libertarian. Hence the very natural processes that operate in animal and plant evolution along the symbiotic lines of participation and differentiation reappear as social processes in human evolution, albeit with their own distinctive traits, qualities, and gradations or phases of development. Coherence takes the form not of a mystical teleology that predetermines the end in the beginning of a process, but of a tendency that is unified by the shared history that society has as a result of its emergence from nature and individuality has as a result of its emergence from society. What would be truly mystical is the notion that social history, which has its ground in natural history, is so severed from its own parentage that nature no longer operates as a basic factor in social development or, for that matter, that an individual's biography is so autonomous that society no longer operates as a basic factor in personal development.

The municipality is close at hand, existential, and ever-present in our lives. The nation-state is remote, largely the product of ideology, and almost ethereal in the ordinary person's experience—except when it invades his or her personal environment with its demands. Our nationality tends to be a media event and our state capitals tourist traps. When we return home from them, we are restored not only to a personal world which we call our "homes," but also a village, town, neighborhood, or city that is the real locus of our lives as social and political beings. The rest is largely synthetic and more contrived than spontaneous. To reflect on these realities of our lives is to break through the fog of nationalist obscurantism and recover not only our sense of place but also our sense of politics. Ecological politics, in this sense, is a politics of *oikos* and community, the ecocommunity in which people live out their social and political lives in a fully existential and ethically meaningful way.

That this environment must recover its human scale, that it must be decentralized sufficiently so that we can understand it and participate in it, is too obvious to belabor. That it must be freed of those statist and economic constraints which inhibit its spontaneous differentiation into a world rich in its diversity of stimuli, the freedom to create, and the opportunity to choose alternatives that make freedom existentially meaningful is equally obvious by now. That citizenship is an ethical compact, not a commercial contract, is a historic truth to which we must repair if we are to be truly human.

The nation-state makes us less than human. It towers over us, cajoles us, disempowers us, bilks us of our substance, humiliates us—and often kills us in its imperial adventures. To be a citizen of a nation-state is an abstraction which removes us from our lived space to a realm of myth, clothed in the superstition of a "uniqueness" that sets us apart, as a national entity, from the rest of humanity—indeed, from our very species. In reality, we are the nation-state's victims, not its constituents—not only physically and psychologically, but also ideologically.

Nothing reveals this more vividly than the extent to which the nation-state has absorbed the energy and belief systems of domestic radical movements. Nearly all of them today have joined the conflict between nation-states and have virtually abandoned their universalist claims to seek human liberation as such. Today they are part of the Cold War and their efforts are deployed in conflicts between "superpowers" and their junior powers in the Third World. Socialism in great part has become a form of national socialism in its quest for national affiliations—its attempt to clothe its ideals or even fit them to meet territorial tangibility and national identity. The deeply humanistic internationalism, indeed *antinationalism*, that characterized radical movements in the early decades of this century and was voiced by revolutionary heroines like Louise Michel and Rosa Luxemburg has been transformed into a crude nationalism that shrilly participates in imperial designs, even as it professes to oppose imperialism as such. Hence the cynical selectivity of the dogmatic "Left": embarrassment with the Russian invasion of Hungary in 1956, virtual silence about the Russian invasion of Czechoslovakia in 1968, near complicity with the war in Afghanistan, and faint motion of "protest" against the crushing of Polish Solidarity in recent years.

The color of radicalism today is no longer red; it is green, and should be raised aloft boldly if the modern crisis is to be resolved. The politics we must pursue is grassroots, fertilized by the ecological, feminist, communitarian, and antiwar movements that have patently displaced the traditional workers' movements of half a century ago. The ethics we need is predicated on a definition of the good, not on calculations of "lesser evils" or "benefits versus risks" that betray us to the worst of evils and the greatest of risks that lie at the end of the road. And the function of our politics must not only be to mobilize, but also to educate, to use knowledge for the empowerment of people, not for their manipulation.

If a green perspective structured around social ecology and its evolutionary vision of freedom does emerge, would it be too bold to say that it will bring together all the threads of the seemingly fragmented development of the past two decades—a development toward the most expansive and coherent expression of liberation we have known up to now? Would it be reasonable to suppose that the civil rights movement, the counterculture, and the New Left of the early and mid-sixties were the soil for the growth of feminism and gay liberation in the latter half of the decade, for environmentalism and later ecologism in the early seventies, for the persisting communitarian and localist movements in both decades that nourished the anti-nuclear, peace, and citizen activism of more recent times—each forming an aspect of a common development with shared roots and expressive of richer phases in the definition and struggle for freedom? We have not tried to interpret the sixties and seventies as a whole, as a rich continuum that has brought out in ever greater fullness the potentiality for freedom that is latent in our era with all its varied and rich articulations. In any case, each such articulation—be it feminist or peace-oriented, countercultural or environmental, communitarian or localist—remains vibrantly structured in the other and exists as part of a whole that can be regarded as a "new social movement," to use the language of the sociologists, not merely a collection of separate movements that academics inventory in their shopping lists of "new causes" or "failed causes."

Much depends on the level of consciousness such a green movement attains. If it confines itself to evocations of the "simple life," with a "biocentricity" that ignores humanity's own unique potentialities, an "anti-humanism" that denies what we *can* be as human beings in the larger world of life, or an anti-rationalism that ignores the organic nature of dialectical reason because it fears the narrow analytic and instrumental reason so prevalent today, then the continuum of the past decades will be broken and this great development of the time in all its phases will be aborted. With such simple intellectual equipment, it will indeed become too simple-minded to be credible and meaningful. In the climate of cooptation and fragmentation of ideas that makes it possible for utterly contradictory ideas and values to exist in the minds of the same individuals as well as the same written works, a due regard for depth and coherence is more necessary today than it has ever been. It is only fair to ask of everyone that he or she *derive* ideas, not merely *collect* them—that there be an explanation of the origins, meaning, development, and direction of ideas, not merely that they be held together with glue and scotch tape.

Finally, if we plan to speak about public issues to the public, we would do well to draw our language from the political culture of the public—not from languages and traditions that are utterly alien to that culture. In America, this political culture stems from a splendid revolutionary tradition marked by a strong libertarian ambience: a reverence for the rights of the individual over those of the state, of the locality over centralized power, of autonomy over dependency, and of self-sufficiency over corporate control. Indeed, to the extent that Americans adhere to a gospel of property, their allegiances have more to do with the individual independence that property confers than the wealth it represents. That reactionary movements have coopted these allegiances is evidence not of their reactionary nature, but of the inability of centralistic forms of socialism, with their emphases on centralism and state controls, to address them in an authentically libertarian way. The success of regressive ideologies is often searing evidence of the failings that burden their self-styled "progressive" counterparts.

An ideological vacuum exists in modern society, and its crisis still persists. It will not be for want of solutions that this condition will remain, but rather for want of the willingness to see what has changed in recent decades that renders traditional "isms" obsolete. The answers are gestating in our body politic; what we lack are the obstetricians who can bring them to birth and the educators who can bring them to maturity.

September, 1985

What is Social Ecology?

We are clearly beleaguered by an ecological crisis of monumental proportions—a crisis that visibly stems from the ruthless exploitation and pollution of the planet. We rightly attribute the social sources of this crisis to a competitive marketplace spirit that reduces the entire world of life, including humanity, to merchandisable objects, to mere commodities with price tags that are to be sold for profit and economic expansion. The ideology of this spirit is expressed in the notorious marketplace maxim: "Grow or die!"—a maxim that identifies limitless growth with "progress" and the "mastery of nature" with "civilization." The results of this tide of exploitation and pollution have been grim enough to yield serious forecasts of complete planetary breakdown, a degree of devastation of soil, forests, waterways, and atmosphere that has no precedent in the history of our species.

In this respect, our market-oriented society is unique in contrast with other societies in that it places no limits on growth and egotism. The antisocial principles that "rugged individualism" is the primary motive for social improvement and competition the engine for social progress stand sharply at odds with all past eras that valued selflessness as the authentic trait of human nobility and cooperation as the authentic evidence of social virtue, however much these prized attributes were honored in the breach. Our marketplace society has, in effect, made the worst features of earlier times into its more honored values and exhibited a degree of brutality in the global wars of this century that makes the cruelties of history seem mild by comparison.

In our discussions of modern ecological and social crises, we tend to ignore a more underlying mentality of domination that humans have used for centuries to justify the domination of each other and, by extension, of nature. I refer to an image of the natural world that sees nature itself as "blind," "mute," "cruel," "competitive," and "stingy," a seemingly demonic "realm of necessity" that opposes "man's" striving for freedom and self-realization. Here, "man" seems to confront a hostile "otherness" against which he must oppose his own powers of toil and guile. History is thus presented to us as a Promethean drama in which "man" heroically defies and willfully asserts himself against a brutally hostile and unyielding natural world. Progress is seen as the extrication of humanity from the muck of a mindless, unthinking, and brutish domain or what Jean Paul Sartre so contemptuously called the "slime of history," into the presumably clear light of reason and civilization.

This image of a demonic and hostile nature goes back to the Greek world and even earlier, to the Gilgamesh Epic of Sumerian society. But it reached its high point during the past two centuries, particularly in the Victorian Age, and persists in our thinking today. Ironically, the idea of a "blind," "mute," "cruel," "competitive," and "stingy" nature forms the basis for the very social sciences and humanities that profess to provide us with a civilized alternative to nature's "brutishness" and "law of claw and fang." Even as these disciplines stress the "unbridgeable gulf" between nature and society in the classical tradition of a dualism between the physical and the mental, economics literally defines itself as the study of "scarce resources" (read: "stingy nature") and "unlimited needs," essentially rearing itself on the interconnection between nature and humanity. By the same token, sociology sees itself as the analysis of "man's" ascent from "animality." Psychology, in turn, particularly in its Freudian form, is focused on the control of humanity's unruly "internal nature" through rationality and the imperatives imposed on it by "civilization"—with the hidden agenda of sublimating human powers in the project of controlling "external nature."

Many class theories of social development, particularly Marxian socialism, have been rooted in the belief that the "domination of man by man" emerges from the need to "dominate nature," presumably with the result that once nature is subjugated, humanity will be cleansed of the "slime of history" and enter into a new era of freedom. However warped these self-definitions of our major social and humanistic disciplines may be, they are still embedded in nature and humanity's relationships with the natural world, even as they try to bifurcate the two and impart a unique autonomy to cultural development and social evolution.

Taken as a whole, however, it is difficult to convey

the enormous amount of mischief this image of nature
has done to our ways of thinking, not to speak of the
ideological rationale it has provided for human
domination. More so than any single notion in the
history of religion and philosophy, the image of a
"blind," "mute," "cruel," "competitive," and "stingy"
nature has opened a wide, often unbridgeable chasm
between the social world and the natural world, and
in its more exotic ramifications, between mind and
body, subject and object, reason and physicality,
technology and "raw materials," indeed, the whole
gamut of dualisms that have fragmented not only the
world of nature and society but the human psyche
and its biological matrix.

From Plato's view of the body as a mere burden
encasing an ethereal soul, to René Descartes' harsh
split between the God-given rational and the purely
mechanistic physical, we are the heirs of a historic
dualism: between, firstly, a misconceived nature as
the opponent of every human endeavor, whose
"domination" must be lifted from the shoulders of
humanity (even if human beings themselves are
reduced to mere instruments of production to be
ruthlessly exploited with a view toward their
eventual liberation), and, secondly, a domineering
humanity whose goal is to subjugate the natural
world, including human nature itself. Nature, in
effect, emerges as an affliction that must be removed
by the technology and methods of domination that
excuse human domination in the name of "human
freedom."

This all-encompassing image of an intractable
nature that must be tamed by a rational humanity
has given us a domineering form of reason, science,

and technology—a fragmentation of humanity into hierarchies, classes, state institutions, gender, and ethnic divisions. It has fostered nationalistic hatreds, imperialistic adventures, and a global philosophy of rule that identifies order with dominance and submission. In slowly corroding every familial, economic, aesthetic, ideological, and cultural tie that provided a sense of place and meaning for the individual in a vital human community, this antinaturalistic mentality has filled the awesome vacuum created by an utterly nihilistic and antisocial development with massive urban entities that are neither cities nor villages, with ubiquitous bureaucracies that impersonally manipulate the lives of faceless masses of atomized human beings, with giant corporate enterprises that spill beyond the boundaries of the world's richest nations to conglomerate on a global scale and determine the material life of the most remote hamlets on the planet, and finally, with highly centralized State institutions and military forces of unbridled power that threaten not only the freedom of the individual but the survival of the species.

The split that clerics and philosophers projected centuries ago in their visions of a soulless nature and a denatured soul has been realized in the form of a disastrous fragmentation of humanity and nature, indeed, in our time, of the human psyche itself. A direct line or logic of events flows almost unrelentingly from a warped image of the natural world to the warped contours of the social world, threatening to bury society in a "slime of history" that is not of nature's making but of man's— specifically, the early hierarchies from which economic classes emerged; the systems of domination, initially of woman by man, that have yielded highly rationalized systems of exploitation; and the vast armies of warriors, priests, monarchs, and bureaucrats who emerged from the simple status groups of tribal society to become the institutionalized tyrants of a market society.

That this authentic jungle of "claw and fang" we call the "free market" is an extension of human competition into nature—an ideological, self-serving fiction that parades under such labels as social Darwinism and sociobiology—hardly requires emphasis any longer. Lions are turned into "Kings of the Beasts" only by human kings, be they imperial monarchs or corporate ones; ants belong to the "lowly" in nature only by virtue of ideologies spawned in temples, palaces, manors, and, in our own time, by subservient apologists of the powers that be. The reality, as we shall see, is different, but a nature conceived as "hierarchical," not to speak of the other "brutish" and very bourgeois traits imputed to it, merely reflects a human condition in which dominance and submission are ends in themselves, which has brought the very existence of our biosphere into question.

Far from being the mere "object" of culture (technology, science, and reason), nature is always with us: as the parody of our self-image, as the cornerstone of the very disciplines which deny it a place in our social and self-formation, even in the protracted infancy of our young which renders the mind open to cultural development and creates those extended parental and sibling ties from which an organized society emerged.

And nature is always with us as the conscience of the transgressions we have visited on the planet—and the terrifying revenge that awaits us for our violation of the ecological balance.

What distinguishes social ecology is that it negates the harsh image we have traditionally created of the natural world and its evolution. And it does so not by dissolving the social into the natural, like sociobiology, or by imparting mystical properties to nature that place it beyond the reach of human comprehension and rational insight. Indeed, as we shall see, social ecology places the human mind, like humanity itself, within a natural context and explores it in terms of its own natural history, so that the sharp cleavages between thought and nature, subject and object, mind and body, and the social and natural are overcome, and the traditional dualisms of western culture are transcended by an evolutionary interpretation of consciousness with its rich wealth of gradations over the course of natural history.

Social ecology "radicalizes" nature, or more precisely, our understanding of natural phenomena, by questioning the prevailing marketplace image of nature from an ecological standpoint: nature as a constellation of communities that are neither "blind" nor "mute," "cruel" nor "competitive," "stingy" nor "necessitarian" but, freed of all anthropocentric moral trappings, a *participatory* realm of interactive life-forms whose most outstanding attributes are fecundity, creativity, and directiveness, marked by complementarity that renders the natural world the *grounding* for an ethics of freedom rather than domination.

Seen from an ecological standpoint, life-forms are related in an ecosystem not by the "rivalries" and "competitive" attributes imputed to them by Darwinian orthodoxy, but by the mutualistic attributes emphasized by a growing number of contemporary ecologists—an image pioneered by Peter Kropotkin. Indeed, social ecology challenges the very premises of "fitness" that enter into the Darwinian drama of evolutionary development with its fixation on "survival" rather than differentiation and fecundity. As William Trager has emphasized in his insightful work on symbiosis:

> The conflict in nature between different kinds of organisms has been popularly expressed in phrases like the "struggle for existence" and the "survival of the fittest." Yet few people realized that mutual cooperation between organisms—symbiosis—is just as important, and that the "fittest" may be the one that helps another to survive.[1]

It is tempting to go beyond this pithy and highly illuminating judgement to explore an ecological notion of natural evolution based on the development of ecosystems, not merely individual species. This is a concept of evolution as the dialectical development of ever-variegated, complex, and increasingly fecund contexts of plant-animal communities as distinguished from the traditional notion of biological evolution based on the atomistic development of single life-forms, a characteristically entrepreneurial concept of the isolated "individual," be it animal, plant, or bourgeois—a creature which fends for itself and either "survives" or "perishes" in a marketplace "jungle." As ecosystems become more complex and open a greater variety of evolutionary pathways, due to their own richness of diversity and increasingly flexible forms of organic life, it is not only the environment that "chooses" what "species" are "fit" to survive but species themselves, in mutualisitic complexes as well as singly, that introduce a dim element of "choice"—by no means "intersubjective" or "willful" in the *human* meaning of these terms.

Concomitantly, these ensembles of species alter the environment of which they are part and exercise an increasingly *active* role in their own evolution. Life, in this *ecological* conception of evolution, ceases to be the passive *tabula rasa* on which eternal forces which we loosely call "the environment" inscribe the destiny of "*a* species," an atomistic term that is meaningless outside the context of an ecosystem within which a life-form is truly definable with respect to other species.*

Life is active, interactive, procreative, relational, and contextual. It is not a passive lump of "stuff," a form of metabolic "matter" that awaits the action of "forces" external to it and is mechanically "shaped" by them. Ever striving and always producing new life-forms, there is a sense in which life is self-directive in its own evolutionary development, not passively reactive to an inorganic or organic world that impinges upon it from outside and "determines"

---

*The traditional emphasis on an "active" environment that determines the "survival" of a passive species, altered in a cosmic game of chance by random mutations, is perhaps another reason why the term "environmentalism," as distinguished from social ecology, is a very unsatisfactory expression these days.

its destiny in isolation from the ecosystems which it constitutes and of which it is a part.

And this much is clear in social ecology: our studies of "food webs" (a not quite satisfactory term for describing the interactivity that occurs in an ecosystem or, more properly, an ecological *community*) demonstrate that the complexity of biotic interrelationships, their diversity and intricacy, is a crucial factor in assessing an ecosystem's stability. In contrast to biotically complex temperate zones, relatively simple desert and arctic ecosystems are very fragile and break down easily with the loss or numerical decline of only a few species. The thrust of biotic evolution over great eras of organic evolution has been toward the increasing diversification of species and their interlocking into highly complex, basically mutualistic relationships, without which the widespread colonization of the planet by life would have been impossible.

Unity in diversity (a concept deeply rooted in the western philosophical tradition) is not only the determinant of an ecosystem's stability; it is the source of an ecosystem's fecundity, of its innovativeness, of its evolutionary potential to create newer, still more complex life-forms and biotic interrelationships, even in the most inhospitable areas of the planet. Ecologists have not sufficiently stressed the fact that a multiplicity of life-forms and organic interrelationships in a biotic community opens new evolutionary pathways of development, a greater variety of evolutionary interactions, variations, and degrees of flexibility in the capacity to evolve, and is hence crucial not only in the community's stability but also in its innovativeness in the natural history of life.

The ecological principle of unity in diversity grades into a richly mediated social principle, hence my use of the term *social* ecology.* Society, in turn, attains its "truth," its self-actualization, in the form of richly articulated, mutualistic networks of people based on community, roundedness of personality, diversity of stimuli and activities, an increasing wealth of experience, and a variety of tasks. Is this grading of ecosystem diversity into social diversity, based on humanly scaled, decentralized communities, merely analogic reasoning?

My answer would be that it is not a superficial analogy but a deep-seated continuity between nature and society that social ecology recovers from traditional nature philosophy without its archaic dross of cosmic hierarchies, static absolutes, and

---

*My use of the word "social" cannot be emphasized too strongly. Words like "human," "deep," and "cultural," while very valuable as general terms, do not explicitly pinpoint the extent to which our image of nature is formed by the kind of society in which we live and by the abiding natural basis of all social life. The evolution of society out of nature and the ongoing interaction between the two tend to be lost in words that do not tell us enough about the vital association between nature and society and about the importance of defining such disciplines as economics, psychology, and sociology in natural as well as social terms. Recent uses of "social ecology" to advance a rather superficial account of social life in fairly conventional ecological terms are particularly deplorable. Books like *Habits of the Heart* which glibly pick up the term serve to coopt a powerful expression for rather banal ends and tend to compromise efforts to deepen our understanding of nature and society as interactive rather than opposed domains.

cycles. In the case of social ecology, it is not in the *particulars* of differentiation that plant-animal communities are ecologically united with human communities; rather, it is the *logic* of differentiation that makes it possible to relate the mediations of nature and society into a continuum.

What makes unity in diversity in nature more than a suggestive ecological metaphor for unity in diversity in society is the underlying fact of wholeness. By wholeness I do not mean any finality of closure in a development, any "totality" that leads to a terminal "reconciliation" of all "Being" in a complete identity of subject and object or a reality in which no further development is possible or meaningful. Rather, I mean varying degrees of the actualization of potentialities, the organic unfolding of the wealth of particularities that are latent in the as-yet-undeveloped potentiality. This potentiality can be a newly planted seed, a newly born infant, a newly formed community, a newly emerging society—yet, given their radically different specificity, they are all united by a processual reality, a shared "metabolism" of development, a unified catalysis of growth as distinguished from mere "change" that provides us with the most insightful way of *understanding* them we can possibly achieve. Wholeness is literally the unity that finally gives order to the particularity of each of these phenomena; it is what has emerged from the process, what integrates the particularities into a unified form, what renders the unity an operable reality and a "being" in the literal sense of the term—an order as the actualized *unity* of its diversity from the flowing and emergent process that yields its self-realization, the fixing of its directiveness into a clearly contoured form, and the creation in a dim sense of a "self" that is identifiable with respect to the "others" with which it interacts. Wholeness is the *relative* completion of a phenomenon's potentiality, the fulfillment of latent possibility as such, all its concrete manifestations aside, to become more than the realm of *mere* possibility and attain the "truth" or fulfilled reality of possibility. To think this way—in terms of potentiality, process, mediation, and wholeness—is to reach into the most underlying nature of things, just as to know the biography of a human being and the history of a society is to know them in their authentic reality and depth.

The natural world is no less encompassed by this processual dialectic and developmental ecology than the social, although in ways that do not involve will, degrees of choice, values, ethical goals, and the like. Life itself, as distinguished from the nonliving, however, emerges from the inorganic latent with all the potentialities and particularities it has immanently produced from the logic of its own nascent forms of self-organization. Obviously, so does society as distinguished from biology, humanity as distinguished from animality, and individuality as distinguished from humanity in the generic sense of the word. But these distinctions are not absolutes. They are the unique and closely interrelated phases of a shared continuum, of a process that is united precisely by its own differentiations just as the phases through which an embryo develops are both distinct from and incorporated into its complete gestation and its organic specificity.

This continuum is not simply a philosophical construct. It is an earthy anthropological fact which lives with us daily as surely as it explains the emergence of humanity out of mere animality. Individual socialization is the highly nuanced "biography" of that development in everyday life and in everyone as surely as the anthropological socialization of our species is part of its history. I refer to the biological basis of all human socialization: the protracted infancy of the human child that renders its cultural development possible, in contrast to the rapid growth of nonhuman animals, a rate of growth that quickly forecloses their ability to form a culture and develop sibling affinities of a lasting nature; the instinctual maternal drives that extend feelings of care, sharing, intimate consociation, and finally love and a sense of responsibility for one's own kin into the institutional forms we call "society"; and the sexual division of labor, age-ranking, and kin-relationships which, however culturally conditioned and even mythic in some cases, formed and still inform so much of social institutionalization today. These formative elements of society rest on biological facts and, placed in the contextual analysis I have argued for, require ecological analysis.

In emphasizing the nature-society continuum with all its gradations and "mediations," I do not wish to leave the impression that the known ways and forms in which society emerged from nature and still embodies the natural world in a shared process of cumulative growth follow a logic that is "inexorable" or "preordained" by a telos that mystically guides the unfolding by a supranatural and suprasocial process. Potentiality is not necessity; the logic of a process is not a form of inexorable "law"; the truth of a development is what is *implicit* in any unfolding and defined by the extent to which it achieves stability, variety, fecundity, and enlarges the "realm of freedom," however dimly freedom is conceived.

No specific "stage" of a process necessarily yields a still later one or is "presupposed" by it—but certain obvious conditions, however varied, blurred, or even idiosyncratic, form the determining ground for still other conditions that can be expected to emerge. Freedom and, ultimately, a degree of subjectivity that make choice and will possible along rational lines may be desiderata that the natural world renders possible and in a "self"-directive way plays an active role in achieving. But in no sense are these desiderata predetermined certainties that must unfold, nor is any such unfolding spared the very real possibility that it will become entirely regressive or remain unfulfilled and incomplete. That the *potentiality* for freedom and consciousness exists in nature and society; that nature and society are not merely "passive" in a development toward freedom and consciousness, a passivity that would make the very notion of potentiality mystical just as the notion of "necessity" would make it meaningless by definition; that natural and social history bear existential witness to the potentiality and processes that form subjectivity and bring consciousness more visibly on the horizon in the very natural history of mind—all constitute no guarantee that these latent desiderata are certainties or lend themselves to systematic elucidation and teleological explanations in any traditional philosophical sense.

Our survey of organic and social experience may stir us to interpret a development we know to have occurred as reason to presuppose that potentiality, wholeness, and *graded* evolution are realities after all, no less real than our own existence and personal histories, but presuppositions they remain. Indeed, no outlook in philosophy can ever exist that is free of presuppositions, any more than speculation can exist that is free of some stimulus by the objective world. The only truth about "first philosophy," from Greek times onward, is that what is "first" in any philosophical outlook are the presuppositions it adopts, the background of unformulated experience from which these presuppositions emerge, and the intuition of a coherence that must be validated by reality as well as speculative reason.

One of the most provocative of the graded continuities between nature and society is the nonhierarchical relationships that exist in an ecosystem, and the extent to which they provide a grounding for a nonhierarchical society.* It is

---

*Claims of hierarchy as a ubiquitous natural fact cannot be ignored by still further widening the chasm between nature and society—or "natural necessity" and "cultural freedom" as it is more elegantly worded. Justifying social hierarchy in terms of natural hierarchy is one of the most persistent assaults on an egalitarian social future that religion and philosophy have made over the ages. It has surfaced recently in sociobiology and reinforced the antinaturalistic stance that permeates so many liberatory ideologies in the modern era. To say that culture is precisely the "emancipation of man from nature" is to revert to

meaningless to speak of hierarchy in an ecosystem and in the succession of ecosystems which, in contrast to a monadic species-oriented development, form the true story of natural evolution. There is no "king of the beasts" and no "lowly serf"— presumably, the lion and the ant—in ecosystem relationships. Such terms, including words like "cruel nature," "fallen nature," "domineering nature," and even "mutualistic nature" (I prefer to use the word "complementary" here) are projections of our own social relationships into the natural world. Ants are as important as lions and eagles in ecosystems; indeed, their recycling of organic materials gives them a considerable "eminence" in the maintenance of the stability and integrity of an area.

As to accounts of "dominance-submission" relationships between individuals such as "alpha" and "beta" males, utterly asymmetrical relationships tend to be grouped under words like "hierarchy" that are more analogic, often more metaphoric, than real. It becomes absurd, I think, to say that the "dominance" of a "queen bee," who in no way knows that she is a "queen" and whose sole function in a beehive is reproductive, is in any way equatable with an "alpha" male baboon, whose "status" tends to suffer grave diminution when the baboon troop moves from the plains to the forest. By the same token, it is absurd to equate "patriarchal harems" among red deer with "matriarchal" elephant herds,

Sartre's "slime of history" notion of the natural world that not only separates society from nature but mind from body and subjectivity from objectivity.

which simply expel bulls when they reach puberty and in no sense "dominate" them. One could go through a whole range of asymmetrical relationships to show that, even among our closest primate relatives, which include the utterly "pacific" orangutans as well as the seemingly "aggressive" chimpanzees, words like "dominance" and "submission" mean very different relationships depending upon the species one singles out and the circumstances under which they live.

I cannot emphasize too strongly that hierarchy in society is an *institutional* phenomenon, not a biological one. It is a product of organized, carefully crafted power relationships, not a product of the "morality of the gene," to use E. O. Wilson's particularly obtuse phrase in his *Sociobiology*. Only institutions, formed by long periods of human history and sustained by well-organized bureaucracies and military forces, could have placed absolute rule in the hands of mental defects like Nicholas II of Russia and Louis XVI of France. We can find nothing even remotely comparable to such institutionalized systems of command and obedience in other species, much less in ecosystems. It verges on the absurd to draw fast-and-loose comparisons between the "division of labor" (another anthropocentric phrase when placed in an ecological context) in a beehive, whose main function is reproducing bees, not making honey for breakfast tables, and human society, with its highly contrived State forms and organized bureaucracies.

What renders social ecology so important in comparing ecosystems to societies is that it decisively challenges the very function of hierarchy as a way of ordering reality, of dealing with differentiation and variation—with "otherness" as such. Social ecology ruptures the association of order with hierarchy. It poses the question of whether we can experience the "other," not hierarchically on a "scale of one to ten" with a continual emphasis on "inferior" and "superior," but ecologically, as variety that enhances the unity of phenomena, enriches wholeness, and more closely resembles a food-web than a pyramid. That hierarchy exists today as an even more fundamental problem than social classes, that domination exists today as an even more fundamental problem than economic exploitation, can be attested to by every conscious feminist, who can justly claim that long before man began to exploit man through the formation of social classes, he began to dominate woman in patriarchal and hierarchical relationships.

We would do well to remember that the abolition of classes, exploitation, and even the State is no guarantee whatever that people will cease to be ranked hierarchically and dominated according to age, gender, race, physical qualities, and often quite frivolous and irrational categories, unless liberation focuses as much on hierarchy and domination as it does on classes and exploitation. This is the point where socialism, in my view, must extend itself into a broader libertarian tradition that reaches back into the tribal or band-type communities ancestral to what we so smugly call "civilization," a tradition, indeed an abiding human impulse, that has surged to the surface of society in every revolutionary period, only to be brutally contained by those purely societal forms called "hierarchies."

Social ecology raises all of these issues in a fundamentally new light, and establishes entirely new ways of resolving them. I have tried to show that nature is always present in the human condition, and in the very ideological constructions that deny its presence in societal relationships. The notion of dominating nature literally *defines* all our social disciplines, including socialism and psychoanalysis. It is the apologia *par excellence* for the domination of human by human. Until that apologia is removed from our sensibilities in the rearing of the young, the first step in socialization as such, and replaced by an ecological sensibility that sees "otherness" in terms of complementarity rather than rivalry, we will never achieve human emancipation. Nature lives in us ontogenetically as different layers of experience which analytic rationalism often conceals from us: in the sensitivity of our cells, the remarkable autonomy of our organ systems, our so-called layered brain which experiences the world in different ways and attests to different worlds, which analytic reason, left to its own imperialistic claims, tends to close to us—indeed, in the *natural history* of the nervous system and mind, which bypasses the chasm between mind and body, or subjectivity and objectivity, with an organic continuum in which body grades into mind and objectivity into subjectivity. Herein lies the most compelling refutation of the traditional dualism in religion, philosophy, and sensibility that gave ideological credence to the myth of a "dominating" nature, borne by the suffering and brutalization of a dominated humanity.

Moreover, this natural history of the nervous system and mind is a cumulative one, not merely a successive one—a history whose past lies in our everyday present. It is not for nothing that one of America's greatest physiologists, Walter B. Cannon, titled his great work on homeostasis *The Wisdom of the Body*. Running through our entire experiential apparatus and organizing experience for us are not only the categories of Kant's first *Critique* and Hegel's *Logic*, but also the *natural history of sensibility* as it exists in us hormonally, from our undifferentiated nerve networks to the hemispheres of our brains. We metabolize with nature in production in such a way that the materials with which we work and the tools we use to work on them enter reciprocally into the technological imagination we form and the social matrix in which our technologies exist. Nor can we ever permit ourselves to forget, all our overriding ideologies of class, economic interest, and the like notwithstanding, that we socialize with each other not only as producers and property owners, but also as children and parents, young and old, female and male, with our bodies as well as our minds, and according to graded and varied impulses that are as archaic as they are fairly recent in the natural evolution of sensibility.

Hence, to become conscious of this vast ensemble of natural history as it enters into our very beings, to see its place in the graded development of our social history, to recognize that we must develop new sensibilities, technologies, institutions, and forms of experiencing that give expression to this wealth of our inner development and the complexity of our biosocial apparatus is to go along with a deeper grain of evolution and dialectic than is afforded to us by the "epistemological" and "linguistic" turns of recent

philosophy.* On this score, just as I would argue that
science is the history of science, not merely its latest
"stage," and technology is the history of technology,
not merely its latest designs, so reason is the history
of reason, not merely its present analytic and
communicative dimensions. Social history includes
natural history as a graded dialectic that is united
not only in a continuum by a shared logic of
differentiation and complementarity; it includes
natural history in the socialization process itself, in
the natural as well as the social history of experience,
in the imperatives of a harmonized relationship
between humanity and nature that presuppose new
ecotechnologies and ecocommunities, and in the
desiderata opened by a decentralized society based
on the values of complementarity and community.

The ideas I have advanced so far take their point
of departure from a radically different image of nature
than the prevailing western one, in which

---

*Our disastrously one-sided and rationalized "civilization" has
boxed this wealth of inner development and complexity away,
relegating it to preindustrial lifeways that basically shaped our
evolution up to a century or two ago. From a sensory viewpoint,
we live atrophied, indeed, starved lives compared to hunters
and food cultivators, whose capacity to experience reality, even
in a largely cultural sense, by far overshadows our own. The
twentieth century alone bears witness to an appalling dulling of
our "sixth senses" as well as to our folk creativity and craft
creativity. We have never experienced so little so loudly, so
brashly, so trivially, so thinly, so neurotically. For a comparison
of the "world of experience we have lost" (to reword Peter
Laslett's title), read the excellent personal accounts of so-called
Bushmen, or San people, the Ituri Forest pygmies, and the works
of Paul Shepard on food-gatherers and hunters—not simply as
records of their lifeways but of their epistemologies.

philosophical dualism, economics, sociology, psychology, and even socialism have their roots. As a social ecologist, I see nature as essentially creative, directive, mutualistic, fecund, and marked by complementarity, not "mute," "blind," "cruel," "stingy," or "necessitarian." This shift in focus from a marketplace to an ecological image of nature obliges me to challenge the time-honored notion that the domination of human by human is necessary in order to "dominate nature." In emphasizing how meaningless this rationale for hierarchy and domination is, I conclude—with considerable historical justification, which our own era amply illuminates with its deployment of technology primarily for purposes of social control—that the idea of dominating nature stems from human domination, initially in hierarchical forms as feminists so clearly understand, and later in class and statist forms.

Accordingly, my ecological image of nature leads me to drastically redefine my conception of economics, sociology, psychology, and even socialism, which, ironically, advance a shared dualistic gospel of a radical separation of society from nature even as they rest on a militant imperative to "subdue" nature, be it as "scarce resources," the realm of "animality," "internal nature," or "external nature." Hence, I have tried to re-vision history not only as an account of power over human beings that by far outweighs any attempt to gain power over things, but also as power ramified into centralized states and urban environments, a technology, science, and rationality of social control, and a message of "liberation" that conceals the most awesome features of domination, notably, the traditional socialist orthodoxies of the last century.

At the juncture where nature is conceived either as a ruthless, competitive marketplace or a creative, fecund biotic community, two radically divergent pathways of thought and sensibility emerge, following contrasting directions and conceptions of the human future. One ends in a totalitarian and antinaturalistic terminus for society: centralized, statist, technocratic, corporate, and sweepingly repressive. The other ends in a libertarian and ecological beginning for society: decentralized, stateless, artistic, collective, and sweepingly emancipatory. These are not tendentious words. It is by no means certain that western humanity, currently swept up in a counterrevolution of authoritarian values and adaptive impulses, would regard a libertarian vision as less pejorative than a totalitarian one. Whether or not my own words seem tendentious, the full logic of my view should be seen: the view we hold of the natural world profoundly shapes the image we develop of the social worlds, even as we assert the "supremacy" and "autonomy" of culture over nature.

In what sense does social ecology view nature as a grounding for an ethics of freedom? If the story of natural evolution is not understandable in Locke's atomistic account of a particular species' evolution, if that story is basically an account of ecosystem evolution toward ever more complex and flexible evolutionary pathways, then natural history itself cannot be seen simply as "necessitarian," "governed" by "inexorable laws" and imperatives. Every organism is in some sense "willful," insofar as it seeks to preserve itself, to maintain its identity, to resist a kind of biological entropy that threatens its integrity and complexity. However dimly, every organism transforms the essential attributes of self-maintenance that earn it the status of a distinct form of life into a capacity to choose alternatives that favor its survival and well-being—not merely to react to stimuli as a purely physico-chemical ensemble.

This dim, germinal freedom is heightened by the growing wealth of ecological complexity that confronts evolving life in synchronicity with evolving ecosystems. The elaboration of possibilities that comes with the elaboration of diversity and the growing multitude of alternatives confronting species development opens newer and more fecund pathways for organic development. Life is not passive in the face of these possibilities for its evolution. It drives toward them actively in a shared process of mutual stimulation between organisms and their environment (including the living and non-living environment they create) as surely as it also actively creates and colonizes the niches that cradle a vast diversity of life-forms in our richly elaborated biosphere. This image of active, indeed striving, life requires no Hegelian "Spirit" or Heraklitean *Logos* to explain it. Activity and striving are presupposed in our very definition of metabolism. In fact, metabolic activity is coextensive with the notion of activity as such and imparts an identity, indeed, a rudimentary "self," to every organism. Diversity and complexity, indeed, the notion of evolution as a diversifying history, superadd the dimension of variegated alternatives and pathways to the simple fact of choice—and, with choice, the rudimentary fact of *freedom*. For freedom, in its most germinal form, is also a function of diversity and complexity, of a "realm of necessity" that is diminished by a growing and expanding multitude of alternatives, of a widening horizon of evolutionary possibilities, which life in its ever-richer forms both creates and in its own way "pursues," until consciousness, the gift of nature as well as society to humanity, renders this pursuit willful, self-reflexive, and consciously creative.

Here, in this ecological concept of natural evolution, lies a hidden message of freedom based on the "inwardness of life," to use Hans Jonas's excellent expression, and the ever greater diversification produced by natural evolution. Ecology is united with society in new terms that reveal moral tension in natural history, just as Marx's simplistic image of the "savage" who "wrestles with nature" reveals a moral tension in social history.

We must beware of being prejudiced by our own fear of prejudice. Organismic philosophies can surely yield totalitarian, hierarchical, and eco-fascistic results. We have good reason to be concerned over so-called nature philosophies that give us the notion of *Blut und Boden* and "dialectical materialism," which provide the ideological justification for the horrors of Nazism and Stalinism. We have good reason to be concerned over a mysticism that yields social quietism at best and the aggressive activism of reborn Christianity and certain Asian gurus at worst. We have even better reason to be concerned over the eco-fascism of Garrett Hardin's "lifeboat ethic" with its emphasis on scarce resources and the so-called tragedy of the commons, an ethic which services genocidal theories of imperialism and a global disregard for human misery. So, too, sociobiology, which roots all the savage features of "civilization" in our genetic constitution. Social ecology offers the coordinates for an entirely different pathway in exploring our relationship to the natural world—one that accepts neither genetic and scientistic theories of "natural necessity" at one extreme, nor a romantic and mystical zealotry that reduces the rich variety of reality and evolution to a cosmic "oneness" and energetics at the other extreme. For in both cases, it is not only our vision of the world and the unity of nature and society that suffers, but the "natural history" of freedom and the basis for an objective ethics of liberation as well.

We cannot avoid the use of conventional reason, present-day modes of science, and modern technology. They, too, have their place in the future of humanity and humanity's metabolism with the natural world. But we can establish new *contexts* in which these modes of rationality, science, and technology have their proper place—an *ecological* context that does not deny other, more qualitative modes of knowing and producing which are participatory and emancipatory. We can also foster a new sensibility toward otherness that, *in a nonhierarchical society*, is based on complementarity rather than rivalry, and new communities that, scaled to human dimensions, are tailored to the ecosystem in which they are located and open a new, decentralized, self-managed public realm for new forms of selfhood as well as directly democratic forms of social management.

November 12, 1984

Market Economy or Moral Economy?

Sooner or later, every movement for basic social change must come to grips with the way people produce the material means of life—their food, shelter, and clothing—and the way these means of life are distributed. To be discreetly reticent about the material sphere of human existence, to loftily dismiss this sphere as "materialistic," is to be grossly insensitive to the preconditions for life itself. Everything we eat to sustain our animal metabolism, every dwelling or garment we use to shelter us from the inclemencies of nature, are normally provided by individuals like ourselves who must work to provision us, as we, one hopes, are obliged to provision them.

Although economists have blanketed this vast activity with amoral, often pretentiously "scientific" categories, preindustrial humanity always saw production and distribution in profoundly moral terms. The cry for "economic justice" is as old as the existence of economic exploitation. Only in recent times has this cry lost its high standing in our notion of ethics, or, more precisely, been subordinated to a trivial place by a supraeconomic emphasis on "spirituality" as distinguished from "materiality."

Accordingly, it is easy to forgive the great German thinker Theodor Adorno for acidly observing a generation ago: "There is tenderness only in the coarsest demand: that no one shall go hungry anymore."[1]

Overstated as this image of tenderness may seem, it is a much-deserved slap in the faces of those privileged strata whose "chubby insatiability" for the good things of life is matched only by their "chubby insatiability" for the contrived problems of their shrivelled and bored egos. It is time—indeed, necessary—to restore the *moral* dimension of what we so coldly denote as "the economy," and more to the point, to ask what a truly moral economy is.

The difficulty in tying economics to morality stems from the nature of economic life as we know it today. Not that any economy can ever really be "amoral" as the economists or practitioners of "economic science" would have us believe, nor, for that matter, can ways of work and technology ever be regarded as "amoral."*

---

*Marx, like David Ricardo, played a major role in divesting economic theory of its moral content and surrounding it with a scientistic ambience even while he denounced capitalism for its brutality and egotism. Marx's *Capital* is riddled with mixed messages that impute the all-presiding, seemingly "just" role to equivalence in the capitalist economy, particularly in the exchange of labor power for wages, while exhibiting a genuine revulsion for an economic system that reduces every human relationship to a cash nexus. Marx's scorn for demands like "economic justice," particularly a "just wage," seems to be almost unknown to most Marxists these days, a scorn which would be laudable were it not the product of his own scientistic image of economics as the study of "the natural laws of capitalist production."[2] For further discussion of the nature of justice, see Chapter V of *The Ecology of Freedom* (Palo Alto: Cheshire Books; 1982).

The fact is that our present market economy is grossly *immoral*. Even in denying that economics can be regarded as an authentically moral domain in which people always make decisions about who shall do what, what shall be distributed to whom, and how "scarce resources" shall be weighed against "unlimited needs," the economists have *literally* "demoralized" us and turned us into moral cretins. Price formation, to take only one example, is not merely an impersonal "amoral" computation of supply versus demand. It is an insidious manipulation of both supply and demand—an immoral manipulation of human needs as part of an immoral pursuit of gain. In speaking of a "market economy" as distinguished from a "moral economy," it would not be false to speak of an "immoral economy" as distinguished from a "moral economy."

But this distinction is hard to see, not only because economics, with its panoply of scientistic pretensions, has muddled the entire issue of economics and morality. It is also hard to see because we tend to assume that the economic status quo is a given, a "natural state of affairs," that is assumed to be part of a fictitious "human nature." So deeply rooted is the market economy in our minds that its grubby language has replaced our most hallowed moral and spiritual expressions. We now "invest" in our children, marriages, and personal relationships, a term that is equated with words like "love" and "care." We live in a world of "trade-offs" and we ask for the "bottom line" of any emotional "transaction." We use the terminology of contracts rather than that of loyalties and spiritual affinities. This kind of business babble, garnished with electronic terms like "input," "output," and "feedback," could easily fill a dictionary for our times and those which lie ahead.

Life, in effect, has acquired those descriptive traits that earlier generations once assigned to strictly market interactions—interactions whose influence on their conduct was marginal, however invasive it became in periods of economic difficulty. The "dignity of labor" denoted the subordinate role of work to the higher moral concerns of the worker's sense of self-esteem, however much this dignity was violated by the harshness of toil and the commanding presence of economic hierarchies. "Respect" was a criterion for transactions of any kind, and figured no less in the claims of the workplace militant than it did in those of the Mafia "Godfather." In many countries on the road to industrialization, workers waged strikes to defend their self-esteem and express their moral solidarity, not only to gain material and social benefits.

Today, we have virtually lost this sense of moral direction because our social map has been completely taken over by the market. Our economic coordinates deny us any of the means for comparing ethical images of the past with the gray "amorality" of the present. As recently as the 1930s, people could contrast the "dog-eat-dog" attributes of the market place with the solidarity of a village-type neighborhood world and its rich supports in the extended family, whose older members formed living recollections of a more caring preindustrial society. Immediately outside the dense, poisoned cities of the world, the countryside was a visible presence, with traditional agrarian lifeways that were hallowed by the ages. However much one may choose to criticize this archaic refuge from the factory, office, and commercial emporium for its parochialism and patriarchialism (a criticism, I can say from personal experience, that has been greatly overstated), the fact remains that it provided a deeply human and personal refuge—one that was fecund with a limitless capacity for renewal and vitality.

Perhaps equally important, it provided "industrial man" with a sense of contrast and tension between a moral world where values of virtue and the good life guided economic standards, and a marketplace world where values of gain and egotism guided moral standards. This sense of contrast and tension was carried inwardly by workers into shop and home, union and family, factory and neighborhood, city and town. Even when the market economy seemed to be the focal center of life during the working day, a sense of an older, more congenial, and moral world to which one could later repair existed in the peripheral vision of the ordinary worker. The space to be a human being with spontaneous human concerns clashed with the space which forced the individual to be a class being, a creature of the market economy and its highly rationalized industrial core.

Ironically, in the vision of millions, the Great Depression of the 1930s moved the market economy from its primary status in the previous decade to a secondary one. Despite the prevalence of a naive commitment to progress and belief in the power of technology to remove all the ills of society, the generation of the early thirties moved in great numbers from the city to the countryside, tightened its family bonds to meet economic adversity, intensified its sense of local solidarity and, with it, neighborhood and town support systems. In short, it recovered moral commitments between people, despite the great dislocations that occurred among farmers in the Dust Bowl and the torrential increase in urban strays who filled the railroad box cars of the middle and far West.

As a result of this parallel movement into and out of the centers of industry and commerce, the impersonal world of frenzied speculation and paper riches so exuberantly celebrated during the boom years of the 1920s suffered a major loss of prestige, as the revival of populist and socialist movements so clearly revealed. The stock market collapse in 1929 ended a popular reverence not only for corporate wealth, but also for the market system itself. Barter, mutual aid, the verities of an agrarian America, self-reliance, and independence, together with regionalism and cultural identity, haunted the land for years and even invaded its artistic canons, as witness the paintings of Grant Wood, the WPA muralists and photographers, and the resurgence of research into local lore and traditions.

Today, this decade-long lapse of the market economy's prestige has simply been forgotten. From the 1950s onward, the market economy has not only imperialized every aspect of conventional life, it has also dissolved the memory of the alternative lifeways that precede it. We are all anonymous buyers and sellers these days, even of the miseries that afflict us. We not only buy and sell our labor power in all its subtle forms, we buy and sell our neuroses, anomie, loneliness, spiritual emptiness, integrity, lack of self-worth, and emotions, such as they are, to gurus, specialists in mental and physical "well-being," psychoanalysts, clerics in all garbs, and ultimately to the armies of corporate and governmental bureaucrats who have finally become the authentic sinews of what we euphemistically call "society." We buy and sell the outward trappings of personality: the sheen-like leather jackets that make humble bookkeepers look like dashing pimps and the high-heeled boots that make bored secretaries look like dangerously seductive whores. Clothing, face paint, well-blown coiffures, baubles, a vast array of insignia and tokens all combine in the urban cesspools of the world to make us seem more "interesting" and less depersonalized than we really are.

Convention submerges in a quick dip only to resurface as stylized indiosyncracies, damning badges of "individuation" that subtly affirm its loss. The snapped cap of the traditional worker, even the high hat of the cartoon bourgeois, once topped faces that were etched with character, experience, inner strength, and individuality. Today the doll-like heads of our "bohemian" middle classes, these relics of a vibrant past, seem like grotesque caricatures. Today the market economy has shown its power to reach the most inward recesses of personality by making its acolytes into look-alikes even as they grasp for the idiosyncratic in dress and the low culture of the mass media. Indeed, whatever is culturally exciting and fills our concert halls and theaters to the bursting point is the recycled product of generations now dead or dying—often recycled with a technical proficiency and slickness that bleeds it of all character and earthiness.

Our liberalism toward every moral excess seems

more like indifference than tolerance. Anomic, spiritless, and unfeeling, we have become the very free-floating commodities we so eagerly produce and devour. Society, in turn, flattened and colorless, has become the very market economy we once confined to the personally remote world of "business." The immorality of our credo of "amorality" stems from a sense of indifference that is evil because it has no criteria for the good and the virtuous. Its philosophy consists of the endless prattle of small talk and its ideals are embodied in its garishly cluttered shopping malls, which have become its most imperious and sacred temples.

The market economy is blessed with a grand secret from which it draws its power to shape the totality of social life: the power of anonymity. Sellers do not know buyers and buyers do not know sellers. What sellers dump on the market—all self-serving myths of "salesmanship" aside—are their commodities, not themselves. A buyer who purchases a dress ultimately confronts an object, a dress—not its producer, a person. Admittedly, there are producers who fit a buyer for a garment and "sales" personnel who oil the purchase along. But the fitter or tailor is a marketplace archaism who actually belongs to a bygone era, or serves a highly affluent elite. The "salesperson" is at best a catalyst for making purchasable dreams more palatable. He or she is virtually nonexistent in the great shopping malls, where the principal encounter between buyer and seller occurs on a checkout line at a cash register, not in the more intimate world where the purveyor of merchandise tries to persuade a potential buyer into a purchase. No, the market economy is structured around buyer and object, or producer and retail establishment, not between person and person.

The anonymity of the exchange process today has formidable consequences, more far-reaching than we normally suspect. We are struck first by its suffocating impersonality. A machine called the market takes over vital functions that rightly should be performed by the intercourse between people. Although electronic and print media continually barrage us with images and voices that seem like human beings, we rarely encounter real flesh-and-blood people in the modern market. Often, no way exists to leisurely discuss the worthiness of a product with the producer who, it would seem, can best judge its qualities and utility. Salespersons, few as they are, are notoriously ignorant about the commodities they purvey and can be easily outwitted by any knowledgeable buyer. Moreover, they are generally outrageously indifferent and excessively rehearsed. They can be—in some places have already been— replaced by a recording. In the impersonality of the market, no interchange between buyer and seller exists that can lend itself to *ethical* guidance.

In all past eras, the worthiness of a product was morally integrated with the worthiness of its seller and producer. The value that a buyer placed on a commodity, indeed, on any exchangeable entity, constituted an ethical gauge of the moral integrity of the individual from whom it was acquired. To denigrate this object, to return it with disparaging remarks about its quality, was to impugn the seller's probity and self-esteem—not simply as a "good" producer, but as a *person* with ethical standards. The craftsperson, in this sense, was as "good" as the "goods" he or she crafted; the seller, as "good" as the "goods" he or she sold. I use the word "good" not instrumentally, in terms of technical proficiency—a word that today, quite characteristically, usually means precisely that—but ethically, in terms of human "goodness" and moral probity. "Good will" meant honesty, integrity, reliability, responsibility, and a high sense of public service, rather than staying power in the marketplace jungle, fiscal soundness, and the contrived myth of "superiority" inculcated in the public mind by advertising. One did not buy a "name" that repeatedly appeared on television screens, neon signs, and billboards; one "bought" the moral certainty of a good personal reputation, an artist's sense of commitment to aesthetic excellence, the cherished *aretē*, or virtue, that the Greeks imputed to an individual's vocation as a moral calling, and the deeply felt responsibility of a good worker to a product that constituted an extension of his or her human powers. "Goods" and "goodness"—a commonality of terms that is not accidental— carried the ethical imprimatur of social responsibility, not the instrumental slickness of technical finesse and hard-sell.

The actual act of selling, in turn, had its own etiquette and personal ambience. Buyer and seller encountered each other with talk about the affairs of the day, personal inquiries and assurances, opinions on a host of public issues, and finally, a mutual interest in the product, with knowledgeable remarks about its components, artwork, and merits. A price was a moral bond, not a mere exchange of "goods" for money. The signature of the producer or seller appeared on the product as well as the bill of sale. People used terms like "just prices," not simply "bargains." Between buyer and seller was an ethical tie that signified their reliance, indeed their dependence, on each other for the needful and good things of life. A high sense of mutuality, based on trust and a shared recognition of faith in a nexus of complementarity for sustaining survival itself, permeated the entire exchange process.

We should not consign such relationships to distant ages like the medieval world. However vestigial in form, they existed as recently as the 1930s, when production, despite its increasingly mass character, was commonly tested in the deeply personal arena of small neighborhood retail shops; in the fitting rooms of garment makers; in cobbler, cigar-making, and bakery shops; and in an endless array of service establishments where work was done under the eyes of the customer and even under the eyes of passing crowds.

Today, the anonymity and depersonalization of the market has almost completely divested the exchange process of this moral dimension. Even in so-called alternative enterprises like organic farms, craft shops, and food cooperatives, the ethical inspiration which presumably gave rise to them has been gravely diluted and threatens to fade away. To the degree that these establishments become "established," they become more entrepreneurial than moral. This is especially true when moral inspiration is confused with material need. An organic farm that is meant merely to satisfy a "need" for "good food" rather than food that is cultivated from a sense of "goodness" and ecological concern—like a "food cooperative" that is meant to provide "good food" at cheap prices—is guided more by need than by ethics. That is to say, it is meant to satisfy a concern that is pragmatic rather than moral.

Ironically, none of these concerns can ever supplant the shopping mall. No organic farm can compete successfully with agribusiness, and no food cooperative can successfully outbid, much less outsupply, a supermarket. The most these "alternative" enterprises can do is to coexist precariously with the giants that tower over them, as mere marginalia that appeal on strictly material grounds to society's fringes, not society at large.

Worse, as practical projects that aim for "efficiency," "high returns," expanded operations, a more "successful" marketing strategy, they begin to objectify their consumers as much as they do the produce they sell. They become merely another impersonal business enterprise whose "goods" are as lacking in "goodness" as those of their larger rivals. Dwarfed by the giants who smirk at their existence and claims, they become food pharmacies for dispensing unpolluted "organic" products instead of pills—the drugs for coping with a social disease, not for preventing or curing it. In short, they become as inorganic, depersonalized, computerized, and cynical as the larger enterprises on whose turf they nibble—dumping grounds for organic foods to meet the therapeutic needs of an increasingly anonymous and inorganic public. The moral aspects of distributing or growing food and other produce are blotted out by considerations of "efficiency" and "success"—the two attributes of capitalistic enterprise that lend themselves to a concern for economic quantity at the expense of ethical quality.

To put the issue bluntly: an organic carrot, a homespun garment, a crafted plank of wood, or a hand-worked leather boot is merely a "thing" that people confront as impersonally in a food cooperative or a craft shop as they do in a shopping mall *if it does not carry a moral message that changes it as an exotic creature of an immoral economy.* The "thing" itself will never give voice to a moral message merely by its quality, ecological pedigree, and usefulness. As wholesome, nourishing, attractive, and free of the pollutants that infect our bodies and tastes as it may be, it does not become a "good" in a moral sense for these reasons alone. Moral "goodness" can come only from the *way* in which people interact between themselves, and the sense of ethical purpose they give to their productive activities. It is through the way "goods" are exchanged or, to state the case more radically, the way exchange is *used* to appropriately distribute them such that "buyer" and "seller" cease to be polarized against each other and are joined in an economic community, united by a fraternal or sororal relationship based on a sense of mutual identification and personal complementarity. Care, responsibility, and obligation become the authentic "price tag" of the moral economy, as distinguished from the interest, cost, and profitability that enter into the "price tag" of the market economy.

Care, responsibility, and obligation, we are told, are "ideological" concepts which have no place in a scientist notion of economics. This criticism points to the very heart of the issues raised by a moral economy. A moral economy—a participatory system of distribution based on ethical concerns—is meant to dissolve the immorality that the modern mind identifies with economics as such. Its goal is to dissolve the antagonism between "buyer" and "seller," to show that in practice both "buyer" and "seller" form a *community* based on a rich sense of mutuality, not on the opposition of "scarce resources" to "unlimited needs." The object exchanged is secondary to the ethical values that are explicitly shared by the participants of a moral economy. For "buyer" and "seller" to care for each other's well-being, for them to feel deeply responsible to each other, and for them to be cemented by a deep sense of obligation for their mutual welfare is to replace a strictly economic nexus with an ethical one—that is, *to turn economics into culture* rather than to visualize it as the "circulation" of things. Where distribution becomes a form of complementarity, it ceases in fact to be economic in the usual meaning of the word and the terms "buyer" and "seller" become meaningless.

Material needs begin to express one of many ways in which claims for things become claims for moral integrity. The "buyer's" expectations begin to expand beyond mere needs to a belief in the "seller's" ability to exhibit the highest moral probity in providing the material means of life. The "seller," in turn, advances his or her goods, and "goodness"—an ethical conviction that the means of life serve to satisfy not only material needs, but also spiritual ones that foster trust, community, and solidarity. The rivalry and seeming independence that pervades the market economy is replaced by reciprocity and interdependence in which distribution with its moral etiquette—like primitive rituals—affirms a sense of unity and shared destiny between its participants. The inequalities conferred by differences in strength, health, age, and skill cease to be the damning stigmas of a specious "equality" that permits each individual to drift on his or her own in a deadening and emotionally blunted pursuit of advantage. To the contrary, they spawn a sense of complementarity and a commitment to compensation that yields the great radical maxim: From each according to his or her abilities, to each according to his or her needs.

These images of a moral economy and its ethical preconditions are not abstractions. They imply concrete institutions and specific forms of behavior. Institutionally, they presuppose a new form of productive community, as distinguished from a mere marketplace where each buyer and seller fends for himself or herself—a community in which actual producers are networked and interlocked somewhat like the old medieval guilds in a responsible support system. In this support system, the producers—be they organic farmers, carpenters, leather workers, jewelers, weavers, clothiers, builders, craftspeople and shop workers of all kinds, indeed, professionals such as physicians, chiropractors, nurses, attorneys, teachers, and the like—explicitly agree to exchange their products and services on terms that are not merely "equitable" or "fair" but supportive of each other. Like all real communities, they form a family that provides for the welfare of its participants as a collective responsibility, not simply a personal responsibility. For example, medical people assume a moral duty to care for the health needs of craftspeople, who in turn assume the task of provisioning the community's physicians, nurses, dieticians, etc. This sense of moral complementarity—this social "ecosystem," so to speak—encompasses all members of the productive community. Price, resources, personal interests, and costs play no role in a moral economy. Services and provisions are available as needed, with no "accounting" of what is given and taken.

"Need," in turn, is moralized in the very profound sense of a shared concern of the giver as well as the receiver, for it becomes important for the producer of a "good" to see to it that the consumer suffers no privation or want for lack of his or her product, indeed, that the "good" is the *best* that can be given to whoever is needful. To go "beyond good and evil," if I may use the title of Nietzsche's provocative work, is to seek excellence for its own sake and, above all, for the community's sake rather than remain trapped in amorality or moral relativism.

"Need" turns from mere want of a "good" into a way of identifying producer and consumer in a caring social bond that is guided not by interest, profitability, and cost, with all their quantitative trappings, but by that ineffable qualitative and disinterested sense of mutual welfare such as we expect in parental and sibling relationships. It is no longer the yearning of one individual for a "good," but a collective funding of desire with the shared expectation that fulfillment is a communal desideratum, just as a lover experiences the joy of the beloved in the very fact that a desire is satisfied.

Inasmuch as virtually every consumer is in some sense a producer, the fictive opposition between consumption and production, with its connotation of the "innocent consumer" who must be protected from the "predatory producer," is eliminated.

That the infirm, elderly, or very young do not seem to belong to such a productive community in the technical sense is perhaps all the more reason to include them fully in its benefits, if only to test continually the moral intentions of such a community—that is, to confront it with an ongoing challenge of its own moral probity and disinterestedness. And yet even the elderly and the infirm, I suspect, will *want* to find a function for themselves in a moral economy, be it simply custodial, clerical, or instructive, depending on their training and background in the more active periods of their lives. The point is that a moral economy exists for moral reasons, not simply for reasons of survival or gain. The good life, materially supported by "goods" that are the messengers of "goodness," is an end in itself: a source of new selfhood and new ways of life; an ongoing education in forms of association, virtue, and decency; a countervailing force to the socially, morally, and psychologically corrosive marketplace and its unbridled egotism.

Such a moral economy has no historical precedents on which to model itself—and, in a very real sense, can only be created by practice and experience, rather than precept and past example. But its architects can draw some inspiration from many so-called primitive communities in which usufruct, not ownership, guided people in the availability of tools and resources.* Possibily, too, they can learn from the democratic guild forms of organization that existed in early medieval townships and from certain cooperative or quasi-religious forms of productive association like the Hutterite and Tolstoyan communes. But these forms of associations are hints, often defective when taken by themselves and useful when selectively pieced together, of what must ultimately be a broader concept of a moral economy for society as a whole. A moral economy, structurally speaking, may for a long time be a marginal example of what the human community as a whole should one day become. But so much that now exists in the center of human affairs formerly developed on their margins that we should not despair that a moral economy can only be peripheral to society today.

Even more fundamental than structure is the problem of behavior. A moral economy, based on shared concern rather than private interest, is no better than the sensibilities it fosters. If our concept of a material "good" comes from a waning sense of moral "goodness," the recovery of the tie between the material and the moral, between "good" and "goodness," recasts our very notion of an economy in a radically new light. It places upon a moral economy the crucial function of developing an economic community into an arena for ethical

---

*The notion of usufruct, the freedom of individuals to appropriate resources merely because they want to use them at a time when the "owner" has no need of them, is too complex to discuss here. For a more thorough and historical examination of the pronciple, see The Ecology of Freedom (Palo Alto: Cheshire Books, 1982), especially pp. 50, 51.

education, as well as a moral system of production and distribution.*

Like the Athenian *polis* of some two thousand years ago, a moral economy must become a school for creating a new kind of citizenship: economic citizenship as well as political, productive citizenship as well as participatory, a place for learning a respect for "things" as products of a fecund nature as well as a center for dedicated work, and the embodiment of a spiritualized physicality as well as a productive domain for creating objects for personal consumption. The "curriculum" for such a school involves a "respiritization" of the work process, the "raw materials" this process shapes, the moral context in which people work together, and the purposes for which they work—this, aside from the more obvious issues of familial, communal, or distinctly pedagogical institutions and politically libertarian forms of self-governance through which

---

*This function has often been sadly overlooked by many food cooperatives which, for a time, were administered by the "cooperators" who did the buying as well as the "staff" which organized the distribution of food. That the need for "efficiency" and the competitive stance in which many such cooperatives were placed with large commercial food emporia ultimately provided some justification for a "tightening up" of their operations goes without saying. What is troubling, however, is that the mentality which the seemingly more concerned administrators of the cooperatives exhibited often differed very little from that which we would expect to find in the manager of a supermarket. "Efficiency" was not merely placed before morality and the educative functions of a food cooperative; the latter simply dropped out of sight completely, as though a food cooperative was a *cheaper* depot for victuals rather than a *cooperative* in any sense of the term.

people are educated. Hence, the economic arena becomes a "school"—as it has always been, more for the worse than for the better—forming the moral character of the individual as well as providing major guidelines for his or her behavior.

This economic image of moral self-development is inseparable from the tools and machines that give it reality. Ecotechnologies, such as small-scale solar and wind-power devices, ecological agriculture, aquacultural techniques, energy-conserving shelters and devices, in short, that entire panoply of so-called appropriate technologies (a term I find difficult to accept because the word "appropriate"—for what?— is too morally ambiguous) should be seen more in terms of their ethical function than their operational efficiency. That we must bring the sun, wind, land, flora, fauna, and the building materials of our shelters into our lives in a new, ecologically oriented way if we are to develop an authentic respect for the natural world, its fecundity, and our dependence on it should be obvious. There is more to ecotechnology than its efficiency and renewability: our metabolism with nature will either be mutually interdependent such that our vision of ourselves will place us firmly *within* the natural world—not "above it"—or we will become its most destructive parasites.

Fundamental to that sense of interdependence is a re-visioning of nature as a moral basis for a new ecological ethics. This moral basis, so suspect to the modern scientistic mind, forms the stuff of social ecology and requires separate discussion. Here it suffices to point out that we will either re-vision nature as a domain of fecundity and development or, in the marketplace mentality, conceive of it as a rank jungle to be savagely exploited as we exploit each other in the buyer-seller relationship. A market economy and a moral economy thus stand counterposed to each other on many different levels: in their images of nature, technology, education, work, the production and distribution of the means of life, community, and "goods" as commodities or the embodiment of "goodness."

Above all, they stand counterposed to each other in the way men and women envision themselves and the ideals they advance for human intercourse—indeed, whether these ideals advance no further than mere survival, with all its narrow technocratic and economistic implications, or rise to the level of life, with its broad ecological and ethical implications. On this score, a market economy and a moral economy raise fundamentally opposed notions of humanity's self-realization and sense of purpose, concepts which define the very meaning of material premises on which our development eventually depends.

July, 1983

An Appeal for Social and Ecological Sanity

We may well be approaching a crucial juncture in our development that confronts us with a historic choice: whether we will follow an alternative path that yields a humane, rational, and ecological way of life, or a path which will yield the degradation of our species, if not its outright extinction.

If this seems like a reckless overstatement, the cry of an aging alarmist who has borne witness to more than half a century of growing ecological and social crises, let us try to assess the kind and scope of the problems that have arisen over the past few decades and the dangers they pose for nearly all complex life-forms, including our own, that have evolved over aeons.

Certainly the possible outcome of a world thermonuclear war, even with existing weapons, has not been exaggerated by the grimmest of our social and scientific forecasters. Biologically, the human beings who survived such a conflict would have good reason to envy the dead. Firestorms, radioactive fallout, hundreds of millions of decaying bodies, the barren landscape, evaporated or condensed lakes, the debris of cities and towns, the hopelessly ill and disastrously wounded—I leave out the grimmest of all predictions, a "nuclear winter" which will blanket the earth with dust and debris that will shut out the sunlight necessary for life on the planet—all, taken together, give us reason to wonder whether the grossly degraded ecology of the earth would be capable of supporting mammals like ourselves in the years that would lie ahead.

What concerns us in the event of such a biocidal holocaust is not the future of the accursed "civilization"—with its bloodless gospel of technocracy, egotism, competition, mass culture, manipulatory rationalism, and, above all, warrior mentality of domination and hierarchy—that will have produced such a terrifying conflict. What concerns us is the future of all remaining complex life-forms as such. For the green world of life which still surrounds us will be replaced by the blackened world of an incinerated biosphere—its atmosphere filled with the stench of the dead, its soil and water polluted by deadly radionuclides, its complex food webs completely shredded with their integrity subverted by disease-bearing organisms and the wild population-explosions of insect infestations. Such a world, all bomb and blast effects aside, would never be one that could sustain the complex plant and animal life forms we know today.

Is such a worldwide thermonuclear war still "unthinkable"? While a nuclear conflict between the United States and Russia may not be inevitable, the fluctuation in tensions between the two "superpowers" makes it impossible to answer this question with reassuring certainty. Elements have entered into the "Cold War" that do not depend exclusively upon economic and political issues.

Rearmament with exotic weapons from neutron bombs to "Star Wars" laser beams has ceased to be a mere quantitative factor by which to measure the use of military "deterrence" as a strategy for a "balance of terror," or, put simply, a "peace" structured around terror. No longer do we have a "dialogue" between the superpowers that centers on "arms reductions"; rather, we hear "concerns" for "arms equity," a term so loose that it provides no limit to arms expansion. And when American rearmament goals alone soar to astronomical levels, such goals become a major factor in fostering the credo, now widely held, that the "balance of terror" will be advanced by war, rather than the earlier credo that war can be prevented by the "balance of terror." Given this derangement in our formulas for "terror" as an instrument of foreign policy, each side in an oncoming thermonuclear war is obliged to decide when it will strike the "first blow"—not if it will do so—lest the military technology of its opponent become too ascendent to avoid "military defeat."

War, in effect, increasingly becomes a decision that is guided by technological considerations, not only social, economic, or imperial ones. It becomes a matter of "survival" rather than a matter of "victory." Rearmament, especially with nightmarishly exotic weapons, tends not to bring foes together at the peace table. It brings them closer together at potential battlefronts in a spirit of mutual fear and paranoia, not mutual power that balances each against the other.

It is the anemic meaning of the very word "balance" that exacerbates this spirit of mutual fear and paranoia. Consider how "Cold War" rhetoric from

American leaders is answered in kind by their Russian counterparts. Talk of "limited nuclear wars" has been answered by heightened talk of "imperialist aggression." Each party to this insane babble must make good its fears to justify its threats, to foster and create episodes that validate its claims—hence, prophecy tends to become self-fulfilling. Following out this logic of "terror," American leaders blame the Russians for Central American insurgency while Russian leaders blame Americans for Poland's Solidarity movement. In both cases, these imputations can easily become excuses for widening conflicts either in Latin America or Eastern Europe— conflicts that reflect the rival imperialist schemes of the two superpowers rather than the genuine aspirations of oppressed peoples in El Salvador and Poland. Liberation struggles thus tend to become absorbed into cold war maneuvers and their authenticity—feared by both superpowers— sacrificed to the strategic needs of blocs on either side of the Iron Curtain. The need for liberation and antiwar movements to free themselves from any association with either one of these cold war blocs becomes a massive effort in raising consciousness, a problem that is exacerbated by the fact that these movements are fighting in mountains and jungles with weapons in hand. Hence, the tragedy of Cuba in the late fifties, of Vietnam in the sixties, and of Nicaragua and El Salvador in the eighties—initially, independent movements that were shrewdly turned into gristmills for cold war politics by the CIA and its White House administrators. May this not be the fate of Eastern European movements for freedom in their response to KGB persecutions and Kremlin propaganda!

To worsen matters, within each camp—West or East—there are always factions that take every threatening claim seriously, if only for opportunistic reasons of domestic supremacy. These claims serve to enhance the power of self-styled "hawks" over self-styled "doves," each of whom rewords Clausewitz's old maxim to read that foreign policy is merely a means for determining domestic policy. Home control often begins to depend upon the rhetoric—and, ultimately, the action—that is applied to world control.

Given the altered meaning of the word "balance" and the use of foreign policy as an instrument of domestic policy, the new qualitative factor that has entered into the arms race renders all talk about "parity" in a "balance of terror" increasingly meaningless. The very "scale" that was once used to achieve such a "balance of terror" tends to be replaced by a foreign policy based on military action—as witness American intervention in Vietnam and Russian intervention in Afghanistan. Challenge and response between the two world powers turns around attempts to anticipate when and where one power will overstep the bounds that were once defined by the "scale." Hence, any "first strike" risks the possibility of becoming a preemptive strike, a thoroughly neurotic "defensive act" to parry an anticipated "offensive act."

Put bluntly: the "negotiators" at various "peace talks" cease to function as "diplomats," just as Adolf Hitler ceased to practice "diplomacy" at Munich in

1938—an event that was merely a prelude to war. Present-day diplomats have become brutish apemen for whom the outbreak of war serves merely to gauge the fortitude of their opponents—their willingness or capacity to respond. Formulas like "limited nuclear war" deal with biocide as mere "forays" that exist militarily outside the grim possibilities of a worldwide catastrophe. Thermonuclear and biological warfare thus threaten to become the means of achieving a "compromise," rather than "compromise" being a means for avoiding such devastating forms of warfare.

A genocidal strategy is, in effect, trivialized into a mere tactical foray. A sophistication of military technology becomes a factor in initiating anticipatory military actions that traditionally were explicable only in terms of historic economic, geopolitical, and imperial interests. The decision to make war can be determined as much by the rhetoric of a belligerent diplomacy, with its roots in domestic factional conflicts, as by serious plans for conquest. The historic motives that once made for war or peace are being replaced by flippant ones—a downgrading of the horrors of modern war, an excessive exaggeration of military engineering innovations, a purely ideological "battle of words" that can easily become a genuine battle of machines and people. Cinematic satires like Dr. Strangelove cease to be mere parodies of a world that can live or die according to the whims of a military commander. They become deadly realities that are more portentous of future events than fears that war will be the result of an "accident" or "nuclear proliferation." Our world rulers, not their lowly subordinates, have trivialized the arms race to such an extent that they can no longer be regarded as the sober custodians of the weapons they have evoked over the past forty years.

II

This historic degradation of international relationships is paralleled by a historic degradation of ecological relationships.

The acid rain that has already wholly or partially destroyed half of Germany's forests, and the lumbering of vast rain forests at the rate of an estimated five million trees daily, are compelling symbols of the ecological devastation that beleaguers our entire environment. We are no longer talking about the dangers posed by our chemically polluted air, water, food, furnishings, workplaces, and communities. Nor are we talking about the dangers posed by nuclear power plants, acid rain, and the debilitating effects of lifeways that accompany a sedentary, congested, stressful, and highly urbanized world for which our evolution as a species has in no way equipped us. What really concerns us is our destiny as a life form and the future of the biosphere itself.

The possible deaths of vast forests, including the tropical rain forests that girdle the earth, speak to crises that threaten the integrity of our entire ecological fabric. The 1980s opened with climatic changes that are as startling and portentous as the causes that may be producing them. An increasingly dense mist of aerosol droplets seems to be hanging over the Arctic regions which, in the view of many scientists, appears to be warming this geographic cradle of our world's climatic system. Taken together with the widespread deforestation that is still under way, we appear to be subverting the very ecological bases of our seasons, temperature ranges, and the delicate thermostatic systems that factor in every aspect of our weather. Increased solar flares and volcanic activity may provide us with handy excuses for explaining the climatic changes that occurred early in this decade in the United States, but they obscure the long-range seasonal alterations that seem to be affecting the basic biogeochemical cycles of our planet. Major irregularities in temperature, precipitation, periods of aridity or excessive rainfall, and corresponding reactions by plant and animal life seem to portend serious climatic crises within a span of a decade that most forecasters a generation ago had put off for centuries if present pollution rates were to continue.*

Industrially and technologically, we are moving at an ever-accelerating pace toward a yawning chasm with our eyes completely blindfolded. From the 1950s onward, we have placed ecological burdens upon our planet that have no precedent in human history. Our impact on our environment has been nothing less than appalling. The problems raised by acid rain alone are striking examples of the

---

*See, for example, my essay "Ecology and Revolutionary Thought," a work written in 1964, later reprinted in my book *Post-Scarcity Anarchism* (Montreal: Black Rose Books; 1972), which projected many of these problems into the far-distant future. This essay, which seemed so extravagant two decades ago because of its hypothetical projections, could now be regarded as an understatement of ecological dislocations that currently confront us.

innumerable problems that appear everywhere on our planet. The concrete-like clay layers, impervious to almost any kind of plant growth, replacing dynamic soils that once supported lush rain forests remain stark witness to a massive erosion of soil in all regionsnorth and south of our equatorial belt. The equator—a cradle not only of our weather like the ice caps but a highly complex network of animal and plant life—is being denuded to a point where vast areas of the region look like a barren moonscape. We no longer "cut" our forests—that celebrated "renewable resource" for fuel, timber, and paper. We sweep them up like dust with a rapidity and "efficiency" that renders any claims to restorative action mere media-hype.

Our entire planet is thus becoming simplified, not only polluted. Its soil is turning into sand. Its stately forests are rapidly being replaced by tangled weeds and scrub, that is, where vegetation in any complex form can be sustained at all. Its wildlife ebbs and flows on the edge of extinction, dependent largely on whether one or two nations—or governmental administrations—agree that certain sea and land mammals, bird species, or, for that matter, magnificent trees are "worth" rescuing as lucrative items on corporate balance sheets.

With each such loss, humanity, too, loses a portion of its own character structure: its sensitivity toward life as such, including human life, and its rich wealth of sensibility. If we can learn to ignore the destiny of whales and condors—indeed, turn their fate into chic clichés—we can learn to ignore the destiny of Cambodians in Asia, Salvadorans in Central America, and, finally, the human beings who people our own communities. If we reach this degree of degradation, we will then become so spiritually denuded that we will be capable of ignoring the terrors of thermonuclear war. Like the biotic ecosystems we have simplified with our lumbering and slaughtering technologies, we will have simplified the psychic ecosystems that give each of us our personal uniqueness. We will have rendered our internal milieu as homogenized and lifeless as our external milieu—and a biocidal war will merely externalize the deep sleep that will have already claimed our spiritual and moral integrity. The process of simplification, even more significantly than pollution, threatens to destroy the *restorative* powers of nature and humanity—their common ability to efface the forces of destruction and reclaim the planet for life and fecundity. A humanity disempowered of its capacity to change a misbegotten "civilization," ultimately divested of its power to resist, reflects a natural world disempowered of its capacity to reproduce a green and living world.

Technology and science, which staked out such sweeping claims to emancipate humanity from the ages-old burdens of ignorance, superstition, and the resistance of a "stingy" nature, have now been turned against humanity itself—creating new myths of "progress," control, expediency, and efficiency. These new myths threaten to bind our species to an ever-darker fate than the one from which it was presumably rescued. Our medical and chemical armamentarium, perhaps the most celebrated of our technical and scientific achievements, rescues us from microbial diseases only to deliver us, as a result of its industrial applications, to so-called degenerative diseases like cancer. The laboratories which save our lives in childhood with their "miracle drugs" dispose of us in mid-adulthood with their carcinogens. It is as though a generation that has been so successfully pulled from the womb to suffer the bitter travails of life in a highly rationalized and emotionally demanding world must quickly be denied the wisdom of age and the fruits of repose by premature death from the so-called diseases of civilization.

If this verdict reflects the "best" technology and science can deliver in its most humanistic aspects, one wonders what judgement can be rendered for the worst—notably, the results of its patently demonic sphere. Its bombs? Guns? Rockets? Robots? Cybernetic equipment? Chemical synthetics? The fruits of its nuclear and genetic probings? With the possible exception of certain diagnostic tools, surgical techniques, anesthetics, and "magic bullets"—and even here, one must exclude the activities of Nazi "experimenters" like Herr Mengele in Auschwitz—no technical or scientific dispensation has done more good for humanity than evil. Technology and science have never blossomed more richly, fully, and fruitfully than in war—the art of killing human beings—with the possible exception of "resource exploitation"—the art of killing nature—often for the purpose of effectively killing more human beings. Here, technology and science join in their most demonic form: the use of nature to destroy people by digging up its hidden stores of uranium for bombs, smelting its ores for guns, applying its laws for obliterating entire cities and ultimately the biosphere itself.

Every genie that has been released from the sacred jars of technology and science emerges with a grateful smile—only to loom over us with a snarl and bared teeth once it has been freed from its confines. Scarcely any technique or fragment of knowledge has been spared from a demonic destiny of killing humankind at a rate that may eventually outpace our species' capacity for procreation. In the twentieth century alone, perhaps 200 million people have been killed either directly or indirectly in wars partly orchestrated by the combined work of the scientist and the engineer. A body of wisdom so inverted that it breeds barbarism rather than civilization, darkness rather than enlightenment, destruction rather than creation, remains even more compelling a challenge to the thinking individual of our times than the concrete problems of thermonuclear immolation.

We of this generation and the past one are not unique in dealing with these issues. Had an Alexander, a Caesar, or a Napoleon—these men whom Hegel knighted "world-historical spirits"— possessed the knowledge of killing that we have today, our species would have suffered its ill-deserved end many generations ago. We have merely created by means of technology and science a killing capacity that they were obliged to attain by means of cunning and "strategy." The same psychic and moral constellation for creating a society oriented more toward death than life has been with humanity for centuries. Few indeed were the men during this long period who were frightened by their own technical imagination for producing the means for mass slaughter—all legends about Leonardo da Vinci's scruples on this score notwithstanding.

So deep-seated a capacity to use technology's malignant power to destroy instead of its benign power to create requires a searching analysis of the moral elements and origins of what we today call "civilization." Here it suffices to emphasize that the "means of production" have now become too powerful—too manipulable by small, idiosyncratic if not crazed elites, too prolific and cancerous in their metastatic growth—to be designed, much less used, as means of destruction. The steel that the Alexanders and Caesars used to dispatch human life, like the black powder that the Napoleons employed for their artillery bombardments, are puny relics of a relatively benign past. They have been replaced by thermonuclear and neutron bombs, nerve gases, lethal microbes and toxins, and unerring delivery systems that can be used intercontinentally to inflict horrendous destruction by only a few psychologically conditioned human robots—and soon, inhuman robots which can be programmed to "declare" war or peace by men whose own sanity and mental stability are highly dubious.

We are passing the point where technical and scientific advances, apart from mere marginalia, hold any promise for human survival and well-being. With the discovery of nuclear bombs, every technical advance seems to be guided or perverted by the pursuit of increased killing power, its purposes barely concealed by token claims that it is meant to "serve" humanity. Hence it is not mere Luddism to say that we would be safer as a species if we could restore a Paleolithic world of flints than if we were to "advance" to a "post-industrial" world of "intelligent robots." Not that the former is a desideratum in itself, but merely that it is less menacing and demonic in a society ruled by moral cretins and emotional brutes.

III

How did we arrive at a condition where thermonuclear immolation or ecological degradation confronts society as a realistic destiny if we do not recover earlier opportunities to divert the trends of technology, science, and a domineering rationalism so facilely expressed by the word "progress"? Have we merely been mistaken in our judgement of humanity as evolving moral and rational animals, moving ever-forward toward the high liberatory ideals of the Renaissance and Enlightenment? Is our species inherently tainted by an irrepressible desire to dominate, to visualize the "Other"—be it nature, woman, ethnic groups, or, quite broadly, our fellow beings—as objects to be manipulated or rivals to be subdued? Is "progress" itself a myth that, by its own self-development, turns into its opposite as regression? Is thermonuclear immolation or ecological degradation the logical fate of a species that has been defective from the start, a species for whom the moral and intellectual trappings of "progress" have concealed a fiercely destructive impulse that has merely found in social evolution the all-powerful tools and means of destruction to tear down the planet?

Or do we have reason to believe that these questions have only limited validity, that they express a sinister departure, comparatively recent in time, from the "mainstream" of human and natural evolution? Do we have reason to hope that human beings have inherently moral and rational qualities that are indeed liberatory, and exist today as a potentiality that can be recovered and realized? Is it a given that the "Other" must be reduced to a mere object of manipulation, or can it exist as an end in itself to be cherished disinterestedly or treated benignly in a caring ecological constellation of living beings? Is there, perhaps, a "mainstream" of progress from which we have diverged like a limb from a tree—an overall movement in the affairs of life and humanity that, lurking in the mists of our history, still holds the promise of new ideals of freedom, love, and highly ethical interaction between human beings and between humanity and nature?

How will we be able to answer these questions, much less understand them, if there are no autonomous thinking people around to formulate them? If we are to answer these questions, we are obliged to step back in history to see if some trend in humanity's evolution held the promise of a truly emancipatory progress. We must try to ascertain if there was another juncture, a branching-off point, of our species and our society from a richly evolving trend toward consciousness and true enlightenment. The dead hand of the past does not lie on the "brain of the living" like a "nightmare," as Marx claimed more than a century ago, nor can sweeping social change "draw its poetry...only from the future"— for there is no future for a humanity that seems to have veered onto a path that threatens its very survival in the absence of radical change in its institutions and sensibility. Quite to the contrary: the "tradition of all the dead generations" which Marx, in his effluvium of nineteenth-century progressivism, hoped to exorcise with the "poetry" of "the future" has yet to be recovered and explored in the light of the dead-end that confronts us. The future as we know it today, whether in the form of socialism or capitalism, has no poetry to inspire us.[1]

The "dead" have not "buried the dead," as Marx had hoped; their remains surround us for good or evil and provide the examples—both good and evil— by which to judge the present and literally recreate a future based on continuity with a humanistic and ecological past, one that will yield a humanistic and ecological society in the century that lies ahead.* Hence we must go backward in time, at least in our consciousness, to determine when and how we "erred" so that we may then regain a lost path that can lead us to a liberatory society.

Perhaps the most comprehensive summary we have of humanity's capacity for aggression and

---

*It is in large part this project of recovery and reexamination that my book, The Ecology of Freedom, was intended to undertake, and the reader should consult it for a more expansive exploration. Although very well received by most critics, a few who have been looking for a computer "printout" rather than a recasting and rediscovery of our oppressive and liberatory traditions—both historical and ideological—have not unexpectedly misunderstood the very design of the book. Accordingly, the reader should be cautioned about the book's principal goals lest he or she lose sight of its function and demands for knowledge about our "civilization."

domination, Erich Fromm's *The Anatomy of Human Destructiveness*, effectively refutes images of our species as inherently oriented toward rivalry and subjugation. After an exhaustive review of ethological, paleontological, anthropological, and early historical data, Fromm concludes that human "destructiveness," indeed rivalry, "is neither innate, nor part of 'human nature,' and it is not common to all men." Quite to the contrary: based on an analysis of some thirty "primitive" tribes, the majority are at best "life-affirmative societies" or "non-destructive aggressive societies," which "are by no means permeated by destructiveness or cruelty or by exaggerated suspiciousness," although at worst they may lack "the kind of gentleness and trust" Fromm finds in "life-affirmative societies."[2]

Politically, in a sweeping and perceptive judgement of humanity's extended periods of social development, Jane Mansbridge in her remarkable and well-documented study of democracy, *Beyond Adversary Democracy*, emphasizes that face-to-face, egalitarian, and consensual democracy ("unitary democracy") based on friendship, in contrast to modern "adversary democracy" structured around representation, hierarchy, and majority rule (itself based on competing interests), "almost certainly has a longer history than any form of government. For more than 99 percent of our history, we human beings lived in hunter-gatherer bands, which in all probability practiced unitary democracy."[3]

If these conclusions are sound—and they can now be supported by a considerable amount of data—we must ask ourselves when and how "civilization" veered away from a largely pacific, egalitarian, and caring ordering of human relationships toward an increasingly aggressive, hierarchical, and adversarial social order—that is, toward societies that have tainted almost every major human achievement with destructive powers and demonically elicited from them their potentiality for coercion and domination. Where were the junctures at which human beings began to employ even seemingly benign technologies, reasoning power, and institutions for oppressive and exploitative ends?

Two periods of social evolution that suggest where the branching-off took place seem to emerge from the mists of the past—one, decisive for the course of human history in general, the other, for the formation of the modern era in its most savage and biocidal forms. The primary juncture involves a sequence of shifts from matricentric to patricentric societies, more specifically, from egalitarian and domestically oriented relationships to hierarchically and politically oriented relationships. These reached their crucial moment with the emergence of the bronze-age warrior. The other, more recent branching-off occurred with the discovery of the "New World." The expanding market economy that developed within late feudal society—rarely benign but, as yet, far from devastating in its social and ecological impact—acquired a rapacity, cruelty, and degree of destructiveness unparalleled by any commercial society before it. Beckoned by the precious metals and wealth of two vast continents— the Indian Americas—European society was thrown into a frenzy of greed and insatiable lust for riches that constituted a complete revolution in human values, goals, and needs—a revolution that still permeates our contemporary culture. Even more than Circe in the *Odyssey*, who turned men into beasts, the virgin Americas became a trough that turned Europeans of all nations into swine. We have not shed the bristles of these legendary beings. Worse, we have developed even sharper teeth and more insatiable appetites than the austere Puritans and tempestuous conquistadores who began to cross the Atlantic five centuries ago.

The factors that drove humanity from an egalitarian world into a hierarchical one, from woman's domestic hearth to man's military battleground, from a sensibility rooted in mutualism to one rooted in rivalry are too complex to examine in detail.* Moreover, surrounded as they are by thick archaic mists, these changes apparently affected only a small fraction of humanity, particularly cultures in the Near East and portions of the Americas. The rest of humanity, sifted out by a process of negative selection, had to be pushed into what we call "civilization" kicking and screaming with revulsion. It suffices to say that once the patriarch dissolved out the mother-imagery of early society with his growing powers of life and death over the clan, and

---

*Here again I must refer the reader to *The Ecology of Freedom*, particularly the opening three chapters, for a more thorough account of the way in which gerontocracies, patriarchy, warriors, priestly corporations, and, finally, the State vastly altered the traditional social landscape of humanity, structured around kinship relationships and tribal institutions. Limits of space make it impossible for me to explore the remarkable ways in which egalitarian institutions and nonhierarchical values were turned against themselves in the very process of humanity's movement out of organic and truly non-domineering social and psychological relationships.

once the warrior acquired control over the material means of life as a feudal or kingly land-magnate—at first as defender of the community from hostile aliens, later as aggressor and expropriator of the community's lands—the world of hierarchy and domination began to permeate the world of an egalitarian and ecological society. Initially, by eroding earlier sensibilities of complementarity and mutual aid, an earnest respect for nature, and the use of the gift as a token of human solidarity; afterwards, by inverting cooperation into competition in the very course of manipulating the traditional form of communal labor to serve the "megamachine" of mass corvée labor, and by degrading the ancient view of nature as subject into a world of "objects" or "natural resources"; finally, by substituting the exchangeable commodity for the solemn gift—through all these inversions and changes, the phoenix of rivalry, already latent in the "Big Man" syndrome of tribal society, rose from the ashes of complementarity and reciprocity. Humanity's richly textured ties of mutualism were turned into the chains of the insensate buyer-seller relationship in which the bargain, with its trappings of profitability, replaced the simple giving and taking of things according to need.

In a world that is fairly innocent of greed and hierarchy—a world in which the very word "freedom" is absent from the vocabulary because it is a universal reality of life—only a far-reaching consciousness of the ills that emerge with the first breaches of its libertarian "social compact" can prevent the logic of domination from totally altering a community's fragile sensibility of mutual aid and respect for human beings and the natural world. Naiveté bears not only the charm of purity, but also a dangerous vulnerability to manipulation. Our children pay this harsh penalty daily as they are "socialized"—and no less was it paid by early human society for its sequence of "elders," patriarchs, warriors, priests, and finally, chieftains, kings, and emperors.

The very troughs that turned men into swine, however, contain the nutrients for armoring men against swinishness. The long and bloody toil of "civilization" over the past ten millennia has brought humanity to the brink not only of mass self-destruction, but quixotically, in its own tortured way, to the brink of acute self-consciousness. The epochal surges of history have removed us from the parochial tribalism of the kin-group into a shared sense of universal humanity in which the torment of peoples far removed from our own community can evoke empathetic sentiments and militant action. The step forward from a self-enclosed folk to a worldwide sense of *humanitas* has added a new species-dimension of concerns to our personal and local concerns.

So, too, lying amidst the technologies of destruction are the technologies of creation that can recover terrains we have already damaged, technologies which can possibly be placed in the service of humanity and nature to foster, rather than degrade, social and natural evolution. The unparalleled opportunity of choosing our own needs, rather than simply bending under the material burden of arduous toil and the lack of means for survival, opens a historically new horizon of time to live creatively, to fulfill our personal and social potentialities as human beings, to lift the sense of "scarcity"—be it mythic or not—from our minds, and to become dignified, secure, and self-assured beings.

Finally, behind us lies the wealth of history itself, the treasure-trove of knowledge—of successes laden with promise and failures laden with fault. We are the heirs of a history that can teach us what we must void if we are to escape immolation and what we must pursue if we are to realize freedom and self-fulfillment. We can discover only too easily what our distant ancestors could never know—the trickery and cunning of elites and power-brokers who induced them to chain themselves in servitude. We can undo not only the chains that bind our limbs, but also the chains that bind our minds. New choral notes answer the trumpets of war and the drumbeats of mass cultures: the notes of a totally emancipated world, free of sexual oppression and mindless inhibition, of ethnic prejudice and ageist neglect, of competitive relationships and the unceasing war between human beings and between humanity and nature, of disempowerment in social life and personal life, of a crudely simplified and brutish selfhood and sensibility—the diminution of people to "human resources" that forms the counterpart of nature conceived as "natural resources."

Such a heritage—indeed, the armor to rescue ourselves from leaders who betray, institutions which enslave, methods which coerce, and sensibilities which domineer—involves the searching study of where we "went wrong" in the course of social evolution ages ago and in more recent times. What we can ascertain from this study is that our gravest departures from the development of humanity and nature toward wholeness and fulfillment are not institutional alone. Coercive as were the temples that replaced the natural shrines and groves of tribal peoples, the brutalizing factories and the lifeless technological imagination that replaced more humanly scaled machines and an aesthetic vision of production, the institutional legacies of domination, whether family or State, that replaced the institutional legacies of freedom—the fact remains that the greatest and most effective modes of coercion stemmed from the prejudices, sense of self, and modes of rationality that brought us into complicity with our self-degradation and the degradation of nature.

The internalization of hierarchy and domination forms the greatest wound in human development and the most deadly engine for steering us toward human immolation. Temples, palaces, factories, yes, even prisons, concentration camps, barracks, police, and the vast legal and executive power of the State, form the flesh and organs that hang on the skeletal structure of our own perverted sensibilities. It was when woman herself agreed to her "inferiority" and supine role of service to man; when peasants formed into the serried, mechanized ranks of soldiers; when the "lowly" accepted their own castehood, classhood, and "station in life"; when men and women ceased to look to themselves and the natural world around them and cast their pleading eyes upward to the Supernature occupied by deities of their own making; when artists viewed themselves as laborers and workers viewed themselves as "hands"; when even the oppressed in "white" skins revelled in their self-conferred "superiority" over the oppressed in more tinted skins that the breaks from a fecund social and natural evolution were completed.

Our step back into the past—all the better to clear-sightedly view our present and future—yields the damning conclusion that we are the unknowing architects of our own servitude. What this means, above all, is that the "revolution" which must "draw its poetry...from the future" must indeed more thoroughly revolutionize humanity than it could have projected a century or even a generation ago. Domination and hierarchy, internalized as sexism, ageism, a manipulative rationality, an envious hatred of other human beings, a passion to "master" nature, and a grasping egotism that arrogantly passes for "individualism" must be exorcised together with the externalized forms of domination and hierarchy that bring "masses" to their knees—or to their mass graves. It is not that past "revolutions" took their inspiration from the depths of the past, but rather that they never went far enough in searching out the depths of the present—the armored sensibilities of rule that yield the fully sculpted institutions of rule.

Domination, be it of nature or human beings, thus unites the great themes of our times: feminism, ecologism, alternative technologies, peace, material security, self-empowerment, community, holistic health, mutual aid, and a sensibility of respect for human beings of all ages and ethnic backgrounds. All are united into a common and coherent focus which we may best call social ecology in its broader theoretical aspects and a libertarian populism in its function as a new social practice. Reinforced intellectually and spiritually by this cohering focus, we can trace back the tormented history of our species from its movement away from the preindustrial world opened by the discovery of the "New World" and still further back from its break with a nonhierarchical world that opened with gerontocracies, patriarchy, and the armored warrior of the Homeric world.

In so tracing back these tangential developments which now threaten our very survival, we can learn from the gross distortions they produced in our own sensibilities and social institutions how to formulate the means for retrieval and advance of our consciousness and practice for achieving a free, ecological society.

IV

If we are obliged to recover our humanity in order to rescue it physically, we must ask unequivocally what methods, forms of organization, and institutions we must develop that will bring us from "here to there," from a society that faces biocide to a society that will fulfill humanity's full potentialities.

The gravest single illness of our time is disempowerment. Even the most media-saturated spectator senses, however dimly or intuitively, that she or he has no power over the events and forces that determine humanity's future. A crude jingoistic "patriotism" may merely signify acquiescence to the superhuman powers that be, a self-deceptive desire to follow in the tow of visible institutional and military strength. It does not exhibit any real conviction that, as mere follower, one has acquired even a scintilla of command or shares in its glories. The ruling elites of the world have killed as many of their devotees as their opponents in wars of conquest or repression. The military graveyards provide no less mute testimony to the tribute paid by the obedient than do the debris of concentration camps to the penalty paid by opponents and "social undesirables." Hence the most jingoistic of "patriots" can hardly claim to have a "fatherland" in his or her own soul. Only the myth that power concentrated in the hands of the few is shared by the many constitutes the balm for an ever-suppurating ulcer of subjugation that the obedient must share, not unlike the soldier whose uniform is both the badge of might and its target on the battlefield.

But to recognize that reempowerment of the individual is one of the most crucial issues of our era raises the question of the ideologies that profess to confer it and the institutions that are meant to achieve it. Here, the so-called revolutionary ideologies of our era—socialism and even canonical anarchism—fall upon hard times. They can be as deceptive in forming a new consciousness as the conventional ideologies of ruling elites. Socialism and canonical anarchism—the "isms" of *homo economicus*, of "economic man"—were born with the emergence of commercial and industrial capitalism. And however oppositional they may be, their underlying assumption that the wage worker is inherently subversive of capital tends in varying degrees to form the counterpart of the very system they profess to oppose. What is perhaps even more ironic today is that their "constituency" is literally being "phased out" with the very industrial structures and industrial classes whose historic aspirations they hoped to voice. The factory itself, not to speak of its industrial proletariat, is being placed on the block of cybernetics and robotics, just as the yeoman-farmer was placed on the block of industrial agriculture and agribusiness two generations ago. If workers' movements of all kinds are today becoming mute or irascibly "perverted," it may be that the vocal chords of the society which cradled them are disintegrating and they can say nothing new in a world whose very vocabulary of change is altering profoundly.

In fact, the socialist and syndicalist proclivity for economic reductionism is now actually obscurantist. It not only shares in the bourgeois tendency to render material egotism and class interest the centerpieces of history, it also denigrates all attempts to transcend this image of humanity as a mere economic being— indeed, as "man the toolmaker"—by depicting them as mere "marginalia" at best, as "well-intentioned middle-class ideology" at worst, or sneeringly, as "diversionary," "utopian," and "unrealistic." "Feed the face, then give the moral," Bertolt Brecht's coarse and contemptuous image of humanity, bears the stigma of the very corruption of radical ideologies that has marked bourgeois society's capacity to infiltrate every area of social life with its contagion of egotism.

Capitalism, to be sure, did not create the "economy" or "class interest," but it subverted all human traits—be they speculative thought, love, community, friendship, art, or self-governance— with the authority of economic calculation and the rule of quantity. Its "bottom line" is the balance sheet's sum, and its basic vocabulary consists of simple numbers. Insofar as men and women wrestle with the system within its economic parameters, they can no more search beyond the issues raised by "class interest" than the entrepreneur can search beyond the issues raised by profit and capital accumulation. Worker and capitalist remain wedded to each other in a community of shared sensibilities and roles, just as hostile mates are bound to each other by a mindless reverence for "the family" and the anxious demands of "the children."

No less mythic than the industrial "class wars" that orthodox radicals believed were swirling around factories—factories that are now in disrepair or in debris—are the strategies spawned by the Age of Revolutions: the barricades, the people in arms, the pealing of the tocsins, the vast crowds marching to drums or besieging palaces, seizing government buildings, paralyzing the movement of troops with railroad strikes and feeding the martyrology of day-dreaming insurrectionaries and terrorists. No longer do the ruling elites oppose Puritan Roundheads with swords and halberds, Minutemen with muskets and toy cannons, sans culottes with black-powder rifles and pikes, Communards with breech-loaders and barricades, Petrograd workers with machine guns and armored cars (those "useful things" which Trotsky wistfully recalled in his History of the Russian Revolution). That entire armamentarium which could pit person against person in street battles has been consigned to the museum of history. Today the conventional weaponry of the ruling elites consists of unbelievably destructive "Gatling" guns, cluster bombs, Mach-3 pursuit planes, heavy bombers, napalm, massive aerial bombs, flame-throwers, a dazzling array of automatic weapons, tanks, and armored vehicles to suit every terrain, recoilless artillery, powerful mortars—in sum, a "merely" explosive arsenal that levelled Beirut primarily from the air and swept into exile the most fully equipped "popular" army from seemingly impregnable positions in an urban area overwhelmingly sympathetic to its cause. Much of this destruction is wrought impersonally, from considerable distances where the combatants are lodged, inaccessible to pleas for aid or the impact of propaganda.

No London in the 1640s, no Boston in the 1770s, no Paris in the 1780s and 1870s, no Petrograd in the early 1900s or Barcelona in the 1930s could have withstood this kind of "conventional" anti-insurgency weaponry for a week. One wonders how any of these cities would have fared had they been victims of nuclear missiles, nerve gas, and possible "particle beams," all of which could be pitted against millions of the most devoted revolutionary "masses" by a handful of cloned zealots, boxed into secret missile sites, underground command centers, or distant space stations. Today the barricade is nothing more than a symbol that, at best, can only test the political stability and resoluteness of advancing conscript troops, just as the terrorist's hand weapons and grenades are hopeless expressions of protest by men and women whose desperation is evidence of their frustration rather than their power.

The "people in arms," like the barricade, merely reinforce the *moral* authority of popular opposition, not the military superiority of large numbers armed with hand weapons who can win their cause by pitting power against power. Their real power, in effect, is spiritual, not material. Their arms reflect their willingness to die in combat rather than live in servitude. While this moral message can shake the fortitude of their opponents and abort their assault on the people, such "insurrectionaries" no longer have the real physical power that belonged to revolutionary peoples of the pre-World War II era, the era that marked the Age of Revolutions.

Civil war waged by "Third World" guerillas in Asia, Africa, and Latin America should not deceive us into regarding them as evidence that the Age of Revolutions has survived post-World War II technology and rearrangement of the traditional classes. Logistically, the greatest shelter these guerrillas have is the very simplicity of their country's material development, a factor that actually brought them into motion in the first place. I refer not only to dispossessed, starving, and terrorized peasants but to the poorly developed roads, the mountains and jungles, the fragile communications systems, the ad hoc bridges, the scattered villages, the paucity of power stations—all of which can be used to thoroughly disorient ill-trained conscript troops, greed-ridden officers, corrupt politicians, and psychotic landlords. When a demolished power station can black out an entire province, a shattered bridge close off transport between entire cities, a dislodged fragment of railroad track immobilize battalions of troops, and a score of burned trucks produce food shortages for an urban area, we are talking of episodes that would be negligible in any industrialized country.

The effectiveness of such "revolutions" stems from the fact that they are products of "material underdevelopment," to use the patronizing language of the Western World, not the heirs of "material progress." They are the remnants of pre-industrial social strata and cultures, not of the presumably "sophisticated" and "hegemonic" classes to which Marxism in particular assigned the task of "changing the world" and creating the poetry of the future. Ironically, where they do succeed, as in Russia, China, and given enough time, Vietnam and Cuba, they tend to adopt all the vulgarities of western industry, agriculture, and even consumerism— vulgarities that can be expected to bring their peoples into even greater servitude to contemporary capitalism than the aerial bombs of their colonial oppressors and the automatic rifles of their comprador rulers. Limited as China's "revolution" may be—more precisely, mythic as it may be in its bizarre mix of Marxian rhetoric with jingoistic nationalism—its undoing may be completed more effectively by Hilton hotels, McDonald hamburger emporia, and color televisions than by any factional purges within its Communist Party.

This raises a second striking feature of "Third World revolutions" that markedly distinguishes them from the classical revolutions of the past. The English, American, French, and even Russian and Spanish revolutions were inspired by the universal ideals of the Reformation and Enlightenment to which they, in turn, substantially contributed. Puritan Roundheads in Cromwell's day asserted the rights of the individual and his or her conscience before god—the authority of a "New Jerusalem" that would redeem humanity as a whole from servitude in any form and advance a faith guided by reason and freedom. Congregationalism, the prevalent religion of the radical Puritans, denied the validity of a sacerdotal hierarchy over "free Englishmen" and in so doing denied hierarchy itself, opposing domination with inalienable natural rights. This notion was not confined to religion. From the congregation, which asserted all-powerful rights over any ministry, it extended into the political sphere in the form of New England town meetings based on face-to-face democracy at the base of social life. These high Reformation ideals found further expression more than a century later in the vision of American revolutionaries, who permeated Puritan ideals with the Enlightenment vision of an Age of Reason guided by thought, science, and technological progress. All of humanity, not merely Americans, would be shown the "light" of a dream based on "life, liberty, and the pursuit of happiness." The utopian side of the American Dream was not the equivalent of later immigrant dreams of a "New World" whose "streets were paved with gold"—a land of material abundance and entrepreneurial promise—but a more austere, ethically motivated world rooted in freedom, reason, individuality, and spiritual regeneration.

The French Revolution offered no less a promise of a rationalistic, scientistic utopia. Its rhetoric of "Liberty, Equality, Fraternity" was imbued with utopistic ideals. If religion is not simply the "opiate of the people" but also the "heart of a heartless world," as the young Marx was to add to his more widely celebrated maxim, so the ideals of the classical "bourgeois" revolutions expressed ancient dreams and aspirations for freedom and modern ideals of a humanity guided by reason.*

No claptrap about mere "superstructural ideology" can permit us to ignore the fact that humanity has a history of ethical development that enjoys an integrity in its own right, often quite autonomous from economic development and even profoundly affecting it. Indeed, all the "bourgeois" revolutions tended to overspill the brim of bourgeois self-interest and transfix the development of capitalism on ideals that the terrified bourgeoisie itself never advanced but only distorted. "Life, liberty, equality, fraternity" are great humanistic goals that haunt the modern era. They are not mere "ideological rhetoric" which the bourgeoisie voiced to conceal its own naked self-interest.

These goals were advanced only at the demand of rebellious farmers in America and the volatile *sans-culottes* in France. In the eighteenth century, "patriotism" did not mean "nationalism." It expressed the new sense of citizenship which humans owed to each other, not to tyrants, and the word "citizen" was to be used by all revolutionaries, including Marx and Bakunin, well into the nineteenth century, just as radicals today use the more party-oriented term, "comrade." Louis XVI, who was compelled to change his title from "King of France" to "King of the French," unwillingly mirrored a new spirit of *humanitarian* ideals rather

---

*I do not accept the view that the revolutions of the 17th and 18th centuries were "bourgeois." That the "bourgeoisie," a highly conservative stratum, benefited from these revolutions does not mean that it caused them or "led" them.

than national ones, which the French people envisioned as a beacon for all of Europe and, they hoped, for the entire world. Such ideals persisted in America and Europe well into the twentieth century, only to be manipulated by fascism and Stalinism alike into a narrow, self-enclosed nationalism that restored "Germany," "Italy," and "Mother Russia" in place of Germans, Italians, Russians, indeed, of Europeans as a whole.

The "Third World revolutions" are nationalist rebellions, not "patriotic" revolutions that speak for humanity. One cannot fault them for their parochial qualities. They have lived under the lash of alien exploiters for centuries. But one cannot deny these limitations out of mere sympathy for their travail. Whatever good they bring to their own people, their solidarity is local or regional, not international or guided by a world vision of freedom. They seek "freedom *from*" colonial and comprador oppressors, not "freedom *for*" their own people in a truly libertarian sense of the term. More often than not, they descend into totalitarian forms of social organization, as witness China, southeast Asia, the Caribbean, and even Central America, living in guarded suspicion of their own people as well as of foreign imperialists. They make very little appeal to reason, science, and technology as emancipatory forces for human development. Instead they tend to emphasize a dogmatic faith engendered by mass propaganda, science as a mere tool for control, and technocracy as a gospel of bureaucratic and technical power. Their economic emphasis, like Brecht's, speaks to real material needs—but it permits them to elude a respect for person, freedom to dissent, and a genuine sense of fraternity and happiness based on human solidarity rather than class interest. Their native people begin to hate them for their ethnic and cultural arrogance, as witness the growing opposition they encounter from Indian peoples, Asian and African tribal communities, and remote mountain villagers who eschew their western pretensions and crass attempts to transform "primitive" peasants and pastoralists into modern "proletarians." This domestic imperialism, so greatly nourished by Marx's own writings, creates "class interests" and conflicts where none need exist, merely because a theory—an "ideology," if you will—acquires supremacy over the realities of traditional lifeways.

Such post-Enlightenment nationalist "revolutions" have very little in common with the classical revolutions that fired the landscape of western society from the 1640s to the 1930s. They articulate the stirring of peoples who are seeking nationhood in a capitalist era when socialism, with its pragmatics of nationalized property, a planned economy, and a centralized state to run it all, has become identified with the new forms of bourgeois corporatism and state capitalism. Yes, as Trotsky observed with the bizarre mixture of clarity and myopia that marred his interpretation of the Russian Revolution, the "law" of uneven and combined development makes it possible for peoples who used bows and arrows a decade ago to leap "forward" to automatic rifles and shoulder-rockets without undergoing the intervening evolution of arms which led from one group of weapons to another. What he forgot to add is that peoples whose national revolutions are accomplished in a decade leap directly from tribal and village cultures to viciously totalitarian and technocratic cultures. The political freedom and republican institutions which might restrain these new governments, as they restrain those of their western would-be masters, are never allowed time to develop.

In fact, these very complex mazes of political freedom and republican institutions make the successes of the "Third World revolutions" possible. We cannot ignore the fact that America, with its massive nuclear arsenal, could have won the Vietnamese War, obliterated Cuba, and could still utterly trample on Central America if it were not prevented from doing so primarily by its republican structure and democratic traditions. Its own utopistic mythology grants freedom to oppositional movements at the base of society and to factional conflicts at its summits. A Hitler, leading a homogenized nation and equipped with a modern nuclear armamentarium, would have simply incinerated southeast Asia had he been obliged to confront the area. With nothing to prevent him from freely exercising his will, he would have reduced Central America and Cuba to a radioactive wasteland just as, with puny weapons and explosives, he left much of western Russia in smoldering ruins, exterminating some twenty million people as his armies retreated into Germany.

What patently prevented America from leaving Vietnam a radioactive desert and Central America an ecological shambles is not any lack of technological power at home or the cunning of guerrilla fighters abroad. One factor—and perhaps one factor primarily—stays the armed might of the American colossus: its own institutional structure, the burdens—ideological and political—of its own great Revolution. The "separation of powers," the limited but effective federal republic, the hallowed "Bill of Rights," even the moral authority of its "Yankee democracy" as exemplified by New England's town meetings and residual two-year governorships have done more to prevent the Pentagon from annihilating its opponents in Asia and Latin America than any saber rattling by the Soviets or the cunning of jungle guerrillas. It is only the institutional chains that limit American military might, taken together with its current susceptibility to world public opinion, that provides any freedom of action to insurrectionaries abroad. Should those chains be removed and that susceptibility be replaced by icy indifference, Hitler and his minions would seem like comic-opera caricatures of warriors against the background of America's technological power to destroy—and Russia's and China's reticence in "involving" themselves in explosive international "entanglements."

V

It is precisely in the sphere of the republican institutions and democratic ethos that an authentic American radicalism can find the nourishment for a reempowerment of the American people and a revitalization of American social and political life.

Here, to use Reaganesque language, lies the "window of vulnerability" of the new totalitarians and militarists in American life. Ironic as it may seem to radicals who have been pastured on the economism of class war, technological growth, and "scientific socialism," be it libertarian or authoritarian, politics must now acquire a "supremacy" over economics, ethics over material interest, the claims of life over the claims of survival if any effective movement for radical renewal and change is to be achieved. Not that they must be counterposed to each other, but that each must be given its proper weight in the new balance of social events. The so-called superstructure, to use the language of Marxian "historical materialism," cannot be seen as an epiphenomenon of the "base" if there is to be any resistance to a market-oriented society that tends to make the ordinary individual, even the self-anointed revolutionary, into a mirror-image of itself. To the extent that *homo politicus* can replace *homo economicus,* and *homo collectivicus* can replace both, humanity still has a chance to rescue itself from a spiritual catastrophe in which social immolation and ecological breakdown will merely provide the shroud for an already decaying corpse.

What this reconnaissance into the real opening of American life means is that all thinking people must participate consciously in the tension between the American Dream conceived as utopia and the American Dream conceived as a huge shopping mall. This tension is compellingly real. Perhaps no people today is more conflicted over its commitment to individual rights, its freedom from governmental control, and its freedom of expression at one end of the spectrum, and its desire to surrender all public responsibility and autonomy to the siren-call of material comfort and the opiates of electronic mass culture at the other end. Within this area of conflict the Right has enjoyed a monopoly of power unmatched by a largely indifferent Left. Herein lies a tragedy of monumental proportions. Still nourished by a classical image of radicalism and tormented by a searing guilt for America's role in the "Third World," American radicals have remained strangers in their own homeland, just like the European immigrants who transferred their own heroic struggles against monarchs, semi-feudal landlords, and corrupt bureaucracies into a world whose concerns differed profoundly from the lands of their origin. The association between the two is closer than American radicals care to recognize. Irish direct action, German Marxism, Italian anarchism, and Jewish socialism have always been confined to the ghettoes of American social life. Combatants of a precapitalist world, these militant European radical immigrants stood at odds with an ever-changing Anglo-Saxon society, initially rooted in yeoman-farmer traditions, communities of urban craftsmen, commercial buccaneers, and straying lawless frontiersmen, whose Constitution had been wrought from the struggle for "Englishmen's Rights," not against feudal satraps.

Admittedly, these "rights" were meant for white men rather than people of color, for Anglo-Saxons rather than Celts, Latins, Semites, and Europe's "riff-raff." But rights they were in any case—universal, "inalienable," and "natural rights" that could have expressed higher ethical and political aspirations than the myths of a "workers' party" or the daydreams of "One Big Union," to cite the illusions of socialists and syndicalists alike. Had the Congregationalist town-meeting conception of democracy been fostered over aristocratic proclivities for hierarchy, had political liberty been given emphasis over *laissez-faire, laissez-aller*; had individualism been given an ethical ideal instead of congealing into proprietary egotism; had the Republic been slowly reworked into a confederal democracy; had capital concentration been inhibited by cooperatives and small, possibly worker-controlled, enterprises; had the rights of localities been rescued from the centralized state; and finally, had the middle classes been joined to the working classes in a genuine people's movement such as the Populists tried to achieve (instead of being fractured into sharply delineated class movements)— in short, had this American vision of utopia supplanted the Euro-socialist vision of a nationalized, planned, and centralized economy, it would be difficult to predict the innovative direction American social life might have followed.*

That this was not to be does not mean that it cannot be. Admittedly, for more than a century American radicalism was largely in the custody of millions of immigrants, most of whom could barely speak English. Radicalism remained a ghetto ideology in all its forms, or was simply unrecognizable to its vast immigrant population when it surged out of Texas into the midwest in its distinctively American populist form. New England democracy, so crucial

---

*"Third World" peoples now face very similar alternatives. Will the Indians in Central America, for example, be free to establish autonomous communities rooted in their rich, pre-industrial, native cultural heritage? Or will they be colonized, ultimately even exterminated, by American-supported feudal juntas and Russian-supported technocratic "Ladinos" who conjointly seek to exploit their labor and resources?

in shaping the most radical forms of the Colonial and Revolutionary eras, slumbered in western Massachusetts, in central and northern New Hampshire, in Vermont, and in Maine—reduced, by sheer prejudice, to a mere village archaism in a world of burgeoning cities. Yet never did American radicals, foreign-born or native, ask why a mass workers' party failed to develop as it had on the European continent, or why socialist ideas never took root outside the confines of the ghettoes in this, the most industrialized country in the world.

But is it an "ideological lag" that explains American "backwardness" in the socialist firmament? Were the "real Americans," as Lenin called them in contrast to the Italians, Jews, and Irish, so distant from the high utopian ideals of humanity over centuries of history? Now that the old European immigrants are virtually gone, their parties disbanded, their periodicals closed, their beautiful roses faded, and even their unruly depression-era children aging, can we perhaps look back and ask where they erred and formed a branch of their own away from the historical flow of the utopistic American Dream as distinguished from the material one they cherished?

Certainly they erred when they believed that the world would be remade by the very industrial workers they so often became—a form of social narcissism that is, perhaps, understandable but now more archaic and certainly more irrelevant than the New England town meetings of which they were totally ignorant. These immigrant socialists and anarchists were largely unionists rather than revolutionary utopians. The rhetoric of the "isms" colored the harsh material interests of their class which a Franklin Delano Roosevelt brought to terms with the interest of capital. Once the reconciliation of wage labor and capital was achieved by the annealing effects of the Second World War, socialism became overtly identified with state capitalism and its parties ceased to be truly oppositional, much less revolutionary. When the last pontiff of American socialism, Norman Thomas, chidingly declared that the "late President Roosevelt adopted most of our ideas," the good Reverend said more than he realized. The New Deal lives on as a program for economic centralization and planning to a greater extent than its most hostile opponents are willing to concede. It is the "Pentagon, Inc.," to use Jessica Savitch's phrase, that has largely taken over the functions that were reconnoitered by Roosevelt's NRA, AAA, WPA, CCC, et al.—that has devoured Norman Thomas's old-time Socialist Party as well. The scenario has been changed in many parts, but the plot is very much the same.

Perhaps even more decisive than the disappearance of the European immigrants and their children is the steady demise of their ideological hope: the industrial proletariat itself. The factory in its traditional form is gradually becoming an archaism. Robots will soon replace the assembly line as the agents of mass industrial production, just as they are expected to replace the typist-secretary-accountant as the agents of commercial activity. Cybernetic devices are even invading agriculture on a scale that threatens the miserable livelihood of the migrant farmworker. In time, even "service workers," from retail clerks to mechanics, may be victimized by so-called intelligent robots and throwaway units, and even governmental employees, so politically vigorous by comparison with their counterparts in the "private sector," face technological extinction.

What is crucial here is that the centerpiece for the immigrant "isms," such as the blue- and white-collar working class, is being "phased out" historically, just as the small farmer and the European immigrant have disappeared from the American social landscape. They and their factories are confronted with the same destiny. In key industrial areas that do remain, the Japanese patronal system with its myth of "employee-employer" cooperation—the "participatory democracy" of multinational corporatism—is replacing even the supine unionism of the previous generation of workers. Hence future generations of industrial proletarians may be a marginal stratum—marking the end of American industrial society as we have known it since the post–Civil War era. The military technology that brought the classical Age of Revolution to an end has claimed the constituency of the classical revolution of modern times—the working class itself.

In so sweeping a confrontation between past and future, where do we stand in the present?

The world we have known over the past centuries is undergoing changes that are unequalled by any we have known since humanity turned from the nomadic ways of hunters to the settled ways of agriculturists. To regard this judgement as an overstatement is to exhibit incredible parochialism in the face of a technological leap that by far exceeds the consequences of the traditional Industrial Revolution with its ensuing urbanism, population growth, ascendency of the industrial bourgeoisie, and profound changes in daily lifeways. Contemporary science has now opened the secrets of matter and life, of the atom and gene. Given this knowledge, technology has scarcely crossed the threshold of an era whose boundaries are utterly unforeseeable. Biotechnics and cybernetics alone could vastly alter the landscape of the mind as we have known it up to now. Yet this technology has merely entered the "Kitty Hawk" stage of the Wright brothers who initiated the flight of heavier-than-air machines, a stage that less than eighty years later seems as far removed from aircraft design and power as does the Bronze Age from the use of tools today.

The social impact these technological developments will produce and the political problems they will create are even more difficult to assess. How a market economy that exchanges wages for labor power can deal with tens of millions of men and women who will be displaced by tractable machines, much less the "intelligent" ones that are now on the drawing boards, raises the specter of vast social dislocations. This may well require an all-encompassing system of surveillance, the elimination of free speech, assembly, the most rudimentary forms of representation, in short, all the rights we associate with the word "democracy"—ultimately, complete militarization and population controls that could well lead to compulsory sterilization, conceivably genocide by calculated starvation if not outright extermination. If such measures had not already been used during this century, we would be hard put to believe that they were possible. Yet they did appear in the 1940s and the aftershock of their use has already worn off in a world inured to mass slaughter, death from hunger, and the ebbing of life by old and exotic diseases. The Four Horsemen of the Apocalypse ride routinely across our planet today, but with very limited promise of redemption.

Given these economic and political premises, the residue of the Republic, the Bill of Rights, and the visions of a democratic commonwealth hang like a millstone on the cybernated, robotized, and genetically engineered society that is aborning in our midst. Two visions of the American Dream have reached searing acuity; the contradiction between the American populist past and its totalitarian future could well become explosive. We can foresee what we want and must defend it, if merely as a reaction against the schemes that are emerging to deal with the imperatives of social control and centralized power. To corporate America, our "agrarian" Republic is worse than "obsolete"; it is an unyielding obstacle to the homogenization and management of the American people. To the emerging elites of a cybernetic America, the breach between the separate branches of government must be "healed" by giving preemptive powers to the executive branch over the legislative and judicial. The western republics of the modern world are being geared to accept a new Caesarism, indeed, a new imperium that potentially, at least, could beggar in its power to control and destroy the most commanding monolithic states in history. To guard against this Caesarist tendency has become the precondition for developing a social agenda for our time. And to ignore an overall trend toward a new Caesarism in the name of a "radicalism" so "purified" of all reality and historical understanding as to yield complete inertness would be capitulation to the powers that be.

Equally important is the need to recreate a democratic public, a body politic committed to the ideals of free expression and the right of every person to formulate social policy. Contemporary urban society and the mass media have subverted the very notion of an active citizenry—the soul of such a body politic. Its decline can be summed up in the most fundamental feature of American life: disempowerment.

Reempowerment presupposes that every individual can feel he or she has control over the decisions that affect our society's destiny. Such a sensibility can only be recreated and fostered by a radical change in the scale of everyday life, a *conscious* endeavor to bring the social environment within the purview of the individual, to render it as comprehensible and understandable as possible. No mere intuitive actions and explosive episodes will do for a society that threatens to replace "primitive" innocence and naiveté with a "sophisticated" cynicism and indifference. Decentralization of decision making, and the institutionalization of the "grass roots" into impregnable structures that are built on a face-to-face democracy, constitute the unavoidable challenges that can form a new, active citizenry in a real participatory democracy. Without this "unitary democracy," democracy of any kind may well disappear. Corporate America cannot assert itself over the existing and potential means of power by hybridizing even republican institutions with totalitarian ones. We do not know whether anything less than complete state control can avoid any threat to the corporate order as such and the deployment of a stupendous technological armory to deal with the problems of a historically new epoch in human relationships.

Despite the erosion of our libertarian institutions over the past few generations, American political life still bears the deep imprints of its revolutionary origins. Mythic or real, individual rights, juridical equality, free expression, and resistance to State encroachment still exercise a powerful hold upon the American mind. This is a genuine reality in its own right, all losses of such values notwithstanding. The ideal of "liberty," however varied its meanings to different citizens, looms over the Caesarist challenge to the Republic as a haunting memory that has yet to be uprooted from our national heritage and our political conscience. *Homo economicus* has not yet completely supplanted *homo politicus*. The "Bill of Rights" and the demands of the great Declaration of Independence for "life, liberty, and the pursuit of happiness" still beleaguer the authoritarians like a ghostly army from the past—a *living* past that can yet be galvanized to recreate an empowered, active citizenry and a democratic body politic.

But how can these ideals be given a palpable form at the base of a society already highly centralized politically and economically? Indeed, a society riddled by spectatorial "citizens" who seem like fair game for the mass media and the political star system?

We encounter here the problem of recovering or revitalizing forms of democratic practice already in existence which lie dormant in a political community. I refer to forms that are still structured around the idea of decentralization and human scale—notably, the municipality as the ultimate source of power, be it the neighborhood assembly in large cities or the town meeting in small communities. The United States has given greater moral authority than any other country today to the "grass roots," a distinctively American expression that stems from our traditional emphasis on local government and our uniquely libertarian revolution. If a radical practice of public reempowerment is to take itself seriously, it must initiate the act of reempowering the citizen in the environment in which he or she is most directly immersed—the neighborhood or town. On this basic level of political and social life, it must try to create at least exemplary forms of public assembly whose moral authority slowly can be turned into political authority at the base of society. It may not be given that such a sequence of steps is practical in every American municipality, much less every region of America. But where it is practical or even remotely possible, it must become the most important endeavor of a new radical populism—a new libertarian populism.

Some of the more impressive examples of this renewal, examples that have acquired great moral influence, have been decisions by Vermont town meetings to demand a nuclear freeze and to withdraw aid from the Salvadoran junta, and, in New Hampshire, to resolve the grave ecological problem of acid rain. These decisions, let it be emphasized, are not local "town issues" which traditionally fall within the province of New England town meetings. They are national and international issues which constitutionally fall within the province of the federal government. Aside from the growing tension such decisions produce between the centralized state and the "grass-roots" locality, the *processes* by which these decisions are made become ends in themselves—not merely means to an end. They create an ambience of popular politics, of participatory citizenship, of active involvement in historic issues. They provide that vital function that self-governance should always fulfill: the process of *educating* the citizen into citizenship and deepening one's sense of selfhood through self-governance. Empowerment, even if only moral in its initial phases, imparts the attributes of a greater sense of public activity in the citizen, of social involvement, reflection, discourse, and decision making—the traits of authentic judgement—not merely the episodic act of delivering one's power, political intelligence, and moral standards into the hands of professional power brokers whose names appear on ballots.

This process of recovery and reempowerment has only just begun—and its beginnings are still largely intuitive in inspiration rather than conscious in intent. If such a project were even advanced without any glimmerings of a reality to support it, it would be dismissed today as "utopian" and "unrealistic." Yet a reality it has, even if only rudimentary and unconscious. If the ruling elites could challenge our credulity with gas chambers, crematoria, and the world of Auschwitz, there is no reason why our credulity should be unshakable in the face of town meetings that have given the nuclear-freeze issue a national scope. To close one's eyes to the latter fact and its civic potentialities while decrying in tremulous voices the former fact and its potentialities smacks of authoritarian dogmatism. Indeed, not only does this sense of reempowerment exist in the town meetings of Vermont, but signs that the meetings themselves can even develop confederal ties have surfaced—a possibility whose discussion must be deferred to a larger study of freedom and its institutions.

What cannot pass unnoticed is that men and women can learn to accept the reality that SS commando units systematically exterminated millions of people, and then so facilely deny that thousands of New Englanders—no less American than themselves—can constitute themselves into face-to-face assemblies, indeed, into a public power, and resolve to oppose the expansion of nuclear weapons, the giving of aid to El Salvador, and the transportation of nuclear wastes on federally funded highways. Here, centralistic social theories and media hype yield a denial of reality that, as dogma, becomes more mythic and misguided than the "archaisms" attributed to authentic reality.

Yet, even when these realities become too apparent to deny, they are often dismissed as "peripheral," just as many canonical radicals dismiss ecological, feminist, peace, and countercultural movements as "marginal." Vermont and northern New England generally are dismissed as the rural "fringes" of a highly centralized and urbanized America in which "most" people live out their futile, desperate, and trivialized lives. It is to the "center" of America, to its "heartland" of giant cities, sprawling suburbs, and belts of agribusiness—we are told—that a radical agenda must be tailored. Perhaps—although it is fair to ask why institutional decentralization, neighborhood organizations, and even face-to-face assemblies are necessarily impossible even in the great megalopolitan "centers" of the country. More often than not, we are likely to find that the insistence upon such "impossibilities" is evidence of ideological prejudices, not of practical obstacles. They express archaic commitments to the creation of "class" organizations—workers' parties—for which the very notion of "community" is as much an affront to their economistic theories of society as the critique of hierarchy is an affront to their organizational concepts.

But what, after all, do words like "center" and "periphery" really mean in the dialectics of social change? What is the "core" and what is the "margin" in the dynamics of human development? German philosophy of the Enlightenment era advanced the often startling but plausible insight that every "center" and "core" is destined to dissolve by the logic of its own development—or, to use more popular language, in the "course of time" as a result of historic forces. No "core" has ever remained so "central" that its destiny is eternally prefigured, just as nothing exists—to paraphrase Spinoza—that isn't fit to perish. Indeed, if we are to find the "cores" that will be "central" to society in the future, we must look precisely to the "periphery" and "margins" of a context where they are gradually emerging. For it is here, at the edges of social evolution, just as in the "ecotones," or the edges of natural evolution, that we encounter the rich variety of forms, sensibilities, and institutions that are likely to supplant and transcend the given "centers" of today.

History has tested this mode of thought repeatedly and furnished us with remarkable examples of its soundness. This is not the place to cite them. They are available in abundance in the social and philosophical literature of our era. Classical Athens, too, was "peripheral" and "marginal" to the great Asian empires that loomed beside it, yet from this remarkable *polis*, its population numerically trivial, emerged a wisdom and an example that have yet to be equalled by any of the great "civilizations" of history. We may not know if the notions and practice of reempowerment, particularly the forms and institutions of a "simpler" past, have the relevance assigned to them here. Social development has a remarkable capacity for using and reusing structures that emerged in the past for goals that belong to the future. Uneven and combined development may give a centrality to seemingly "archaic" institutions in remote places like Vermont that can become the decentralized, humanly scaled structures for reempowering the American people as a whole. That such remote places have already served as the cutting edge for social advances elsewhere in the country is demonstrable in the peace and ecological movements.

By the same token, "class analyses" have a way of ossifying into restrictive dogmas that, "central" as they may seem, can be as disorienting as they can be clarifying. If we are to hunt up a "hegemonic class" that will be the "agent" of revolutionary change, we would do well to discard the exclusivity imparted to the industrial proletariat. Historically, it has always required a radical intelligentsia (in no way to be confused with "intellectuals" and academics) to catalyze revolutionary change. Leaving this issue aside, I have argued elsewhere that the very existence of the proletariat as a revolutionary "agent" depends, quixotically enough, on its transcendence as an industrial and purely class creature, not as the class counterpart to capital.* But more significantly, today, this class has rarely adopted the "historic role" assigned to it by radical theorists of all kinds. Worse, it is being "discarded" by contemporary changes in technology. Indeed, if the community is emerging as particularly relevant, this is partly because the factory is losing its eminence as an arena for social change. Community, the locus of radical activity bipolar to the factory, has become increasingly significant largely because the factory has become less significant.

We arrive at still another significant issue: What, after all, is the historical "agent" for sweeping social change? A "new proletariat" of intellectuals, scientists, engineers, technicians, and students who can somehow meld their "economic interests" with those of the Japanese-model assembly line? Blacks, ethnics generally, and/or women? Even in the course of listing these new "strata," we essentially "phase out" the traditional proletariat and traditional "class analyses" from our social inventory, an inventory that was anchored in a clearly definable economic relationship to the traditional bourgeoisie—that is, in specific "production relationships" that were marked by the exchange of labor power for wages and by classes which crossed swords in the conflict

---

*For an account of this argument, see my *Toward an Ecological Society* (Montreal: Black Rose Books; 1980), p. 259.

between "wage-labor and capital." The "new classes" we now deduce are united more by cultural ties than economic ones: ethnics, women, countercultural people, environmentalists, the aged, the déclassé, unemployables or unemployed, the "ghetto" people—all defy the economistic "class analyses" that underpinned Marx's "scientific socialism" and its most successful practitioners like Lenin and Trotsky. A cultural fare of alienation, fear (whether for one's personal security or the "fate of the earth"), frustration, rootlessness, lack of coherence and a meaningful life, aesthetic defilement, and, above all, a powerlessness unite them into those surging demonstrations, broad coalitions, networks, cooperatives, collectives, and social and cultural projects more than any clearly focused economic motivations, significant as these may be. It is this "counterculture" in the broadest sense of the term, with its battery of alternative organizations, technologies, periodicals, food cooperatives, health and women's centers, schools, even barter-markets, not to speak of local and regional political coalitions, that seems to offer serious opposition to the Caesarist and technocratic society that may lie in the offing.

Let us call this remarkable déclassé phenomenon by its real name: the reemergence of "the People." Redolent as the word may be of the "bourgeois-democratic" revolutions of the past, particularly the American and French, the fact remains that it, too, has become recreated by a strange dialectic of negation in which the historic dialectic, to rephrase Theodor Adorno, seems to keep faith with a logic of contrareity that culminates "in its origin."[4] Yet what better word more adequately describes this classless "class," this strangely mixed "mob," whose definition in economic terms consists precisely in its indefinability, whose goals are so culturally—or counterculturally—anchored, whose agenda consists of the utopian slogans of the great democratic revolutions in a common resistance to Caesarism and corporatism.

The reemergence of "the People," in contrast to the steady decline of "the Proletariat," verifies the ascendancy of community over factory, of town and neighborhood over assembly line. The hand fits the glove perfectly—and clenched, it makes the real fist of our time that can advance by restoration, progress by conserving the radicality of the past, change by the catalytic act of preserving the very institutions Caesarism seeks to fragment and corporatism seeks to obliterate. Such tension—once it fully emerges between the locality and centralized State, the citizen and power broker, the body politic and bureaucracy, democracy and totalitarianism—can never remain strictly defensive.

Once locality, citizen, body politic, and democracy assert themselves in popular assemblies, the latter must either confederate on regional levels or face extinction. Once, or if, confederation is achieved, the skein of municipal linkages must be broadened on a national scale or it will atrophy and disappear. Thereafter, its future is hidden in the mists of a logic that can only be established concretely—that can only be revealed when a relationship of forces between the federation of municipalities and the State comes into being. Will this relationship yield confrontation or surrender? By whom and by what means? Peaceful or violent? Conscious or intuitive?

To these questions there are no answers because the issues in all their finality have not yet emerged.

This much is clear: if these issues arise only intuitively, the movements they foster will be betrayed. There is no room for naiveté any longer. The Caeserists and corporatists are too sophisticated, however quarrelsome they may be, to be outmaneuvered by innocents. Their acute consciousness must be answered by a consciousness of our own. Such a consciousness presupposes the learning, study, discussion, debate, teachers, and organizers that can only be supplied by a coherent network of groups whose dedication to social change is single-minded in practice and utterly respectful of mind in theory. Whether the German Greens provide us with an example of such a network or not we have yet to ascertain. If nothing else, we can learn as much from their errors as from their successes. But a Green network we certainly require—one that speaks to Americans in their own tongue, not in European, Asian, or Latin languages and formulas. It must also be one that is spawned from American radical traditions: Yankee democracy, frontier individuality, a popular mistrust of governmental power, a dedication to "grass-roots" democracy, in short, a libertarian populism that is built on the reemergence of "the People" and the institutionalization of the "grass roots" by confederated popular assemblies.

The term "libertarian" itself, to be sure, raises a problem, notably, the specious identification of an anti-authoritarian ideology with a straggling movement for "pure capitalism" and "free trade." This movement never created the word; it appropriated it from the anarchist movement of the last century. And it should be recovered by those anti-authoritarians—whether socialistic or anarchic—who try to speak for dominated people as a whole, not for personal egotists who identify freedom with entrepreneurship and profit. It would be wiser to simply ignore this specious movement for "liberty" and restore in practice a tradition that has been denatured by new disciples of Adam Smith.

Lest the word "libertarian" be seen as a political capitulation to statism, we would do well to realize a flaw in the authentic libertarian tradition that confuses politics in its *Hellenic* sense with statecraft. The traditional libertarian counterposition of "society" to "the State" is not false as such. Social forms like families, clans, tribes, guilds, workshops, village communities, neighborhoods, and towns are the organic institutional forms by which humanity "naturally" developed toward consociation and by which it metabolized with nature in the form of production. It is within these forms that the great anarchic theorists hoped to structure a confederal libertarian society. The State, quite soundly, was seen as an exogenous institution—a professionalized class instrument of executives, legislators, bureaucrats, soldiers, judges, and police with their paraphernalia of barracks, courts, and prisons. This exogenous institution had to be consistently bypassed in daily social activity and disbanded in periods of sweeping social change.

For the present, however, what should be emphasized is that the historical landscape is composed of more than society and the State. We must move beyond this simplistic and Manichean dualism to focus on a generally unexplored arena of human activity, a public space or *political* arena in the classical Hellenic sense of the word *politika*, or activity of the *polis*, that cannot be subsumed by the word State, much less "city-state." Perhaps for the first time in history, but by no means the last, the Athenian democratic *polis* produced an entirely new institutional arena—an arena that was not specifically "social" like the family, clan, tribe, presumably workplace, and various "natural" forms of consociation like clubs, cultic communities, vocational collegia (later, "guilds"), and professional societies. Nor was this institutional arena identical to—or even an extension of—that class-controlled professionalized system of violence such as armies, police, bureaucrats, judges, legislators, and centralized executives we call "the State"—a constellation of structures which were few enough in Periclean Athens although they were quite common in the ancient world.

What the Athenian *polis* created was a uniquely *civic* sphere—a distinctly municipal arena—characterized by the *agora*, or civic center, where citizens could gather informally, discuss, trade, and engage in a richly textured interaction that prepared them for the weekly meetings of all the citizens in the *ecclesia*, or popular assembly, where they normally discussed the issues of the *polis* with a view toward arriving at a public consensus in a face-to-face manner, either with unanimity or by a vote. There, too, as in the *agora*, they were daily and subtly educated into the arts and attributes of active citizenship, or more precisely, into the sensibility, character-structure, and selfhood of participatory and self-governing citizens—a new, specifically municipal "class" in the spectrum of "classes" which Marx and our current bouquet of radical social theorists have so neatly arranged for us. The Athenian democracy, in effect, functioned as a school for personal and social development, and with its dramas, festivals, and pageants provided a unifying *cultural* milieu that knitted together the *polis* into a community unified in sensibility and tradition. Economic strata Athens had in abundance: slaves, craftpersons, merchants, alien residents, or *metics*, who enjoyed none of the political rights of citizens—although there were free, independent farmers, tenant farmers, intellectuals who practiced what we today would call "professions," nobles of aristocratic lineages, and, finally, a stratum of demagogues who tried to manipulate the citizen body to suit their own personal and social interests.

But there was also the citizen body itself—the body politic—that, despite its mixed "class" character, often transcended its particularistic economic interests to arrive at an ethical consensus. This consensus was guided by a notion of the "public good," a "good" that cannot be dismissed as purely "ideological" or subtly class motivated, but which rested on a shared notion of what was transparently the public welfare, all particularistic frictions and conflicts aside. As expressed by the social philosophers of Greece, whether democratic or authoritarian, this notion of the "public good" consisted of the body politic's *aretē*, or virtue. In the Athenian democratic *polis*, politics, or *politika*, to use a safely Hellenized term, belonged neither to the realm of the "social" nor that of the "State," terms for which the Greeks significantly had no words. It comprised the realm of the *polis*, of the *civis*, to use a more familiar Latin word, in which men (the society, like all those around it, was firmly patricentric) formed a "social compact" or common *ethical* understanding—in no way to be confused with a juridical "social contract"—to order its life as a "commonweal" to try to transcend particular interests.

What the anarchic theorists have not seen clearly is a supra-social level of politics—literally, the activity of the *polis*—that can validly be distinguished from *statecraft*. Politics is the public realm of citizenship where citizens gather to discuss social problems, evaluate them, and, finally, decide on their solution, whether by consensus or by vote. This political arena, as distinguished from the largely social world of organic relationships at one end of the spectrum and the statist world of ruling-class controls at the other end, is the intermediate world of the community and the citizen—a municipal world based not on kin but on the *civic* association that so often surfaces in the writing of Proudhon and Kropotkin, only to be overlaid by the industrial world of syndicalism.

Tragically the liberatory side of community and municipal politics was never fully elaborated. Indeed, it was myopically subsumed by an "antipolitical" bias that brought the distinctions caused by statist and social infiltration into a twilight zone of radical social theory. Libertarian municipalism was further stigmatized by the crude betrayals of its most outstanding spokesman, Paul Brousse, the French anarchist who drifted in his later life toward conventional party politics. Cleansed of this stigma, libertarian municipalism *and* its politics, based on popular assemblies and confederal relationships, can be seen as a process that does not deny politics in its *classical* sense but rather serves to give it authenticity and contemporary relevance.

To be sure, recovered forms and structures like town meetings and neighborhood assemblies do not of themselves yield the reempowerment of the citizen, the body politic, and a democratic society, much less the ecological society we hope to achieve. The bottles are no better than the wine they contain. That wine, it is self-evident, must be fermented by a libertarian populist movement, a network or coalition of the classless "class." It must be guarded from pollution by a coherent, highly conscious theory and practice. No less than the theorists and organizers, it must be abetted by events—by contemporary history itself—which unite seemingly single issues into a nexus of general ones and enlarge their logic into historic programs for sweeping social change.

Thus the social movement outside must combine with the intellectual movement inside. Already, feminism tends to meld with ecologism under the common theme of the domination of nature. Countercultural lifeways tend to unite with political movements for freedom, all the more because restrictions on sexual life, behavior, medical strategies, midwifery, art, and perhaps even dress threaten to undermine the very ingredients of culture as such, not to speak of one "counter" to prevalent mores. Even the peace movement cannot confine itself to such single issues as the nuclear freeze, arms reduction, or opposition to relocation plans in the event of war. It is destined to face the fact that it is not just opposed to armaments, but to *militarism*. This old demand, which predates the outbreak of the First World War, has reappeared as a result of the encroaching Caesarist and corporate State and of the militarization of every facet of life from school to industry, from family to community, from sexual relations to social relations. The Pentagon is no longer merely the "command post" of the nation. It threatens through its vast command of resources and the allocation of funds to become the artificial heart of an increasingly bionic and militarized society.

However summarily these remarks have been advanced, they offer a theory and practice for social and ecological sanity. If they have not explored the issue of property rights and multinational corporatism, of imperialistic designs and the problems of nuclear war, of feminism and ethnic oppression, it is only because these issues have been fully explored in countless statements, articles, and books. Civic entities can "municipalize" their industries, utilities, and surrounding land as effectively as any socialist state. The difference would be that a municipally managed enterprise would be a worker-*citizen* controlled enterprise meant to serve human and ecological needs, not a bureaucratically and politically controlled enterprise that assumes an interest and ends of its own. Even more can be said about the replacement of the nation-state by the municipal confederation, the treatment of sexes and "strangers," and the like. To "touch every base" merely to signify one is aware of "every" issue would be hypocritical and manipulative. What I have advanced is a perspective that is different from those which normally appear in most radical social theories—a libertarian populism based on municipal freedom and confederation. This perspective speaks more directly and traditionally to American conditions than the immigrant "isms" that still linger on among radical sects and European traditions of radicalism. It makes no attempt to imperialize the ideological landscape—and it carries the warning that ages long past, both in American history and European, may be irrecoverable for people whose very spirit may be industrialized and reduced to spectatorial passivity.

If nothing else, however, it tries to speak to a more independent, politically concerned, and libertarian American spirit that may still lie latent in the national character-structure. And if nothing is left of that spirit, radicals may follow their own personal course, perhaps returning to the daydreams of dignity in defeat with the certain knowledge that defeat will end in biocide. But if something of that spirit is still left, even as embers, these remarks may be regarded as part of an effort to raise up the flames of protest and provide us with the means for reconstruction.

Here, at least, is a chance for humanity to regain its sanity and rebuild this ruined planet as a world for life. It is a chance that must arouse the very unconscious of the individual and redeem the spirit of life with which he or she was born to produce a new culture and consciousness, not only a new movement and program.

March 19, 1983

Endnotes

Rethinking Ethics, Nature, and Society

1. G.P. Maximoff, ed., *The Political Philosophy of Bakunin* (Selected Writings) (Glencoe, NY: The Free Press, 1953), 358.

2. G.W.F. Hegel, *The Phenomenology of Mind*, Baillie translation (New York: Humanities Press, 1910), 79.

3. Karl Marx, *The Grundrisse*, McLellan translation (New York: Harper & Row, 1972), 94.

4. Jules Michelet, *History of the French Revolution* (Chicago: University of Chicago Press, 1973), 444.

5. Jean-Jacques Rousseau, *The Social Contract* (New York: E.P. Dutton & Co., 1950), 94.

What Is Social Ecology?

1. William Trager, *Symbiosis* (New York: Van Nostrund Reinhold Co., 1970), vii.

Market Economy or Moral Economy?

1. Theodor Adorno, *Minima Moralia* (London: New Left Books, 1974), 156.

2. Karl Marx, *Capital* (New York: Modern Library, 1906), 13.

An Appeal for Social and Ecological Sanity

1. The quotations in this paragraph are drawn from Karl Marx, *The Eighteenth Brumaire of Louis Napoleon*, in Karl Marx and Friedrich Engels, *Selected Works*, Volume 1 (Moscow: Progress Publishers, n.d.), 400.

2. Erich Fromm, *The Anatomy of Human Destructiveness* (New York: Holt, Rinehart and Winston, 1973), 181, 169.

3. Jane Mansbridge, *Beyond Adversary Democracy* (New York: Basic Books, 1980), 10.

4. Adorno, *Minima Moralia*, 157.

About the Author

Murray Bookchin was born in New York City in January 1921 and was involved in the radical and labor movements of the 1930s. For more than thirty years he has been a prophetic spokesman for the ecology, alternate technology, antinuclear, and peace movements. An activist in the new left as well as the old, he was deeply involved in the civil rights movement and counterculture of the 1960s. His influence has been worldwide, and his writings have been translated into all major European languages. One of the theorists of the German Greens, he is currently active in the Green movement in the United States. Director Emeritus of the Institute for Social Ecology, and Professor Emeritus of Ramapo College of New Jersey, he lives in Burlington, Vermont, where he teaches for the Institute and does most of his writing. He is the author of nine previous books, including *Our Synthetic Environment* (1962), *Post-Scarcity Anarchism* (1971), *The Limits of the City* (1973), *Toward an Ecological Society* (1980), and *The Ecology of Freedom* (1982). His forthcoming books are *Urbanization Without Cities* and *The Ethics of Evil*.

About the
Institute for Social Ecology

The Institute for Social Ecology in Rochester, Vermont, is a not-for-profit educational and research institution that was co-founded by Murray Bookchin and Daniel Chodorkoff in 1974. A pioneering and internationally distinguished body, the Institute has instructed nearly two thousand students in its general summer and graduate programs, many of whom are currently engaged in educational and practical work in the field of social ecology. Known for its early efforts to promote alternate technologies, the Institute is particularly outstanding for its message that our ecological problems are rooted primarily in social problems—notably, the domination of human by human that, in turn, has given rise to the notion that humanity can dominate the natural world. This message, structured around a critical evaluation of the emergence of hierarchy and its role in the past and present, advances the reconstructive goal of a new sensibility and an ecological society that will reconcile human with human in a network of new, humanly scaled, decentralized, and rounded communities—communities that will be sensitively integrated into the natural ecosystems in which they are located. Additional information about the Institute can be acquired by writing to P.O. Box 384, Rochester, VT 05767.

More Resources from New Society Publishers

**AFRICA IN CRISIS: THE CAUSES,
THE CURES OF ENVIRONMENTAL BANKRUPTCY**
by Lloyd Timberlake/Earthscan

Consciousness about the African famines has reached an all-time high. Yet awareness about the causes of famine has hardly advanced at all. Winner of the $10,000 World Hunger Media Award for "Best Book" dealing with hunger issues, *Africa in Crisis* demonstrates that though drought may have *triggered* the famines, human mismanagement *caused* them—through unsound agricultural, development and environmental strategies, short-sighted international monetary practices, increased military conflict, and bankrupt foreign aid policies. *Africa in Crisis* also suggests new strategies which could reduce and eventually eliminate Africa's vulnerability to famine.

Published in cooperation with the International Institute for Environment and Development, London and Washington, DC.

240 pages. Illustrated. Photographs. Bibliography. 1986.
Hardcover: $29.95
Paperback: $9.95

Available from your local bookstore or, to order directly, send check or money order to **New Society Publishers**, 4722 Baltimore Avenue, Philadelphia, PA 19143. For postage and handling, add $1.50 for the first book and 40¢ for each additional book.

"If in the future we want to live lives at all fit for human beings, or even if we just want to survive, we must fundamentally change our way of life."

BUILDING THE GREEN MOVEMENT
by Rudolf Bahro

Rudolf Bahro has emerged in recent years as a leading figure in the West German Green Party and a political and social thinker with substantial international influence. In *Building the Green Movement*, Bahro sets forth his views on North-South relations and the peace movement, his opposition to a coalition between Greens and Social Democrats, his increasing disaffection with parliamentary politics, his ideas for the renewal of communities, and his insistence on the need for spiritual resurgence.

"Those familiar with historic radical literature will recognize in Bahro's rhetoric and reasoning the visions of William Morris's *News from Nowhere*, Paul Goodman's "practical proposals," and Ernest Callenbach's *Ecotopia*, not to mention the Taoist precepts of Lao Tzu."

—*Booklist*, American Library Association

224 pages. 1986.
Paperback: $9.95
Hardcover: $29.95